# ADVANCED ARCHITECTURAL MODELMAKING

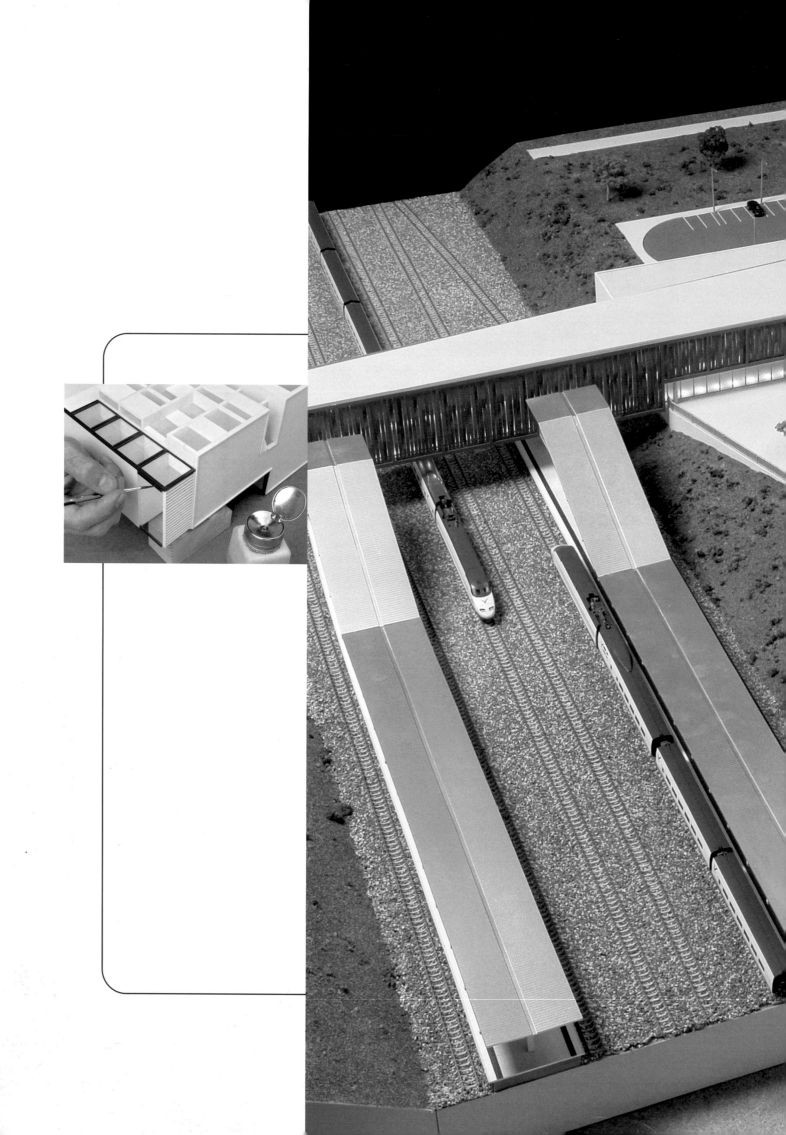

# ADVANCED ARCHITECTURAL MODELMAKING

Eva Pascual i Miró
Pere Pedrero Carbonero
Ricard Pedrero Coderch

**W. W. Norton & Company**
**New York • London**

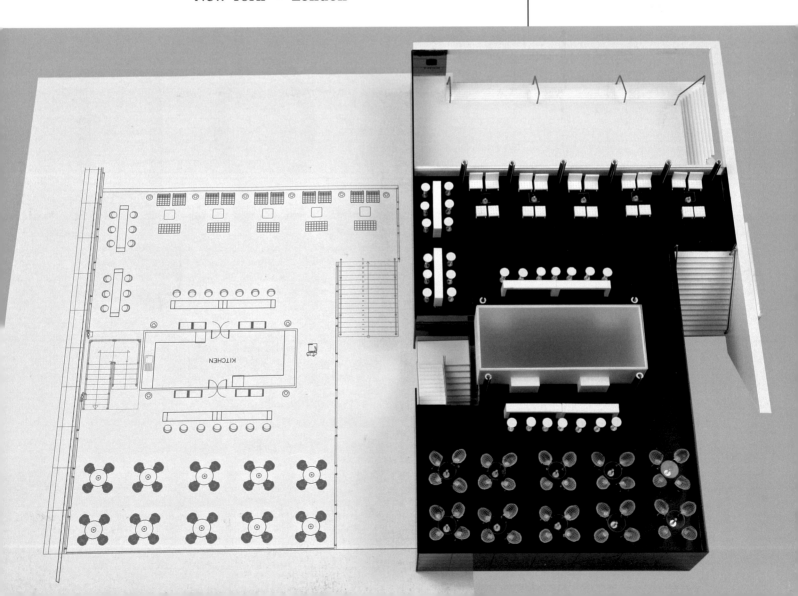

For information about permission to
reproduce selections from this book,
write to Permissions,
W. W. Norton & Company, Inc.,
500 Fifth Avenue, New York, NY 10110

For information about special discounts
for bulk purchases, please contact
W. W. Norton Special Sales at
specialsales@wwnorton.com
or 800-233-4830

Composition by Joe Lops
Production manager: Leeann Graham

Library of Congress
Cataloging-in-Publication Data

Pascual i Miró, Eva.
 [Maquetismo. English]
 Advanced architectural modelmaking /
Eva Pascual i Miró, Pere Pedrero
Carbonero, Ricard Pedrero Coderch.
    p. cm.
 Originally published: Maquetismo.
Barcelona, Spain : Parramón Ediciones,
2009.
 Includes bibliographical references
and index.
 ISBN 978-0-393-73338-9 (pbk.)
1.  Architectural models.  I. Carbonero,
Pere Pedrero. II. Coderch, Ricard Pedrero.
III. Title.
 NA2790.P2813 2011
 720.22'8—dc22
                        2010013111


ISBN: 978-0-393-73338-9 (pbk.)

W. W. Norton & Company, Inc.,
500 Fifth Avenue, New York, N.Y. 10110
www.wwnorton.com

W. W. Norton & Company Ltd.,
Castle House, 75/76 Wells Street,
London W1T 3QT

0 9 8 7 6 5 4 3 2 1

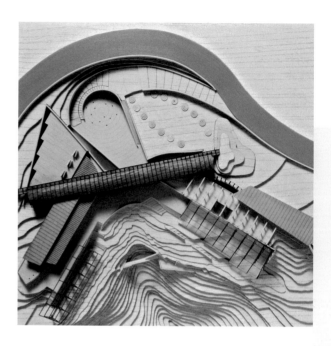

ents

# Introduction

Architectural modelmaking is a discipline that consists of representing a design, construction, or architectural project at a reduced scale and in three dimensions. Architectural models directly derive from the representation of an initial architectural design, and from plans or documents relating to the construction or work that needs to be done. The discipline includes two separate aspects that may at first seem very different, but that are inextricably linked when making any kind of architectural model. The first concerns the technical environment. This involves an understanding of plans and documents, and the conversion of scales and measurements. The elements that are to make up the building and the other parts that make up the model also have to be decided upon. The second aspect refers to the artistic environment, in other words, to the resources used to produce a model. This includes the skills and knowledge that the architectural modelmaker must take into account to perform within the technical environment, but should also include the artistic resources needed for a model's aesthetic components. This helps create an architectural model that is illustrative and comprehensible while being attractive. Both aspects come together when making a model as a representation of reality or an architectural project, but with its own aesthetic and artistic values. Architectural models are in fact a first-class expressive resource. They enable the use of a wide range of materials and finishes, bring about new representations with innovative results accompanied by interesting aesthetic components, and offer unbeatable opportunities to develop creativity. They are also the ideal testing ground for investigating new physical and material solutions.

This book shows the key techniques used to create architectural presentation models. Working models are not discussed here, as strictly speaking they are part of the design definition process of architecture, and this goes beyond the aims of this book. Here, the creation of models has focused on the use of acrylic as a basic material, due to its ease of use and its potential to affect the final result. All of the processes, resources, and solutions explained can be easily extrapolated and applied to other materials. A comprehensive table is therefore included that gives information on the types of adhesives and their uses. The key processes involved in modelmaking and the most common solutions, are also included. We have to bear in mind that each model is unique, always involving new processes and solutions that may be completely different when compared to other projects. So, the specific aspects of each case will be examined.

The book is divided into four main sections. The first explains the basic characteristics of architectural models as a form of representation. The next discusses the materials and tools used in the different techniques. The third looks at the technical processes involved, first theoretical aspects and then the main techniques. The last section is the most extensive, in the form of a step-by-step guide that shows the entire procedure involved in creating five different types of architectural models.

The intention is not to create a definitive manual on making architectural models, but rather to offer a rigorous and clear examination of the key aspects of a technical discipline that has strong artistic components, so that interesting and innovative results can be achieved.

**Pere Pedrero Carbonero** received a technical associated degree at the Escola del Treball in Barcelona. He worked for a watchmaker and then in a workshop specializing in architectural models, where he started his career in this discipline. He has owned his own workshop since 1975, which is involved in major projects for prestigious architecture firms, as well as various public and private institutions.

**Ricard Pedrero Coderch** studied cabinetmaking at the Escola Politècnica dels Salesians de Sarrià and interior design at the Escola Superior de Disseny BAU, both in Barcelona. He worked as a specialist cabinetmaker for several restoration workshops before becoming involved with various theater and television set design companies. He currently works with his father, and both are partners of their own workshop.

**Eva Pascual i Miró** has degrees in art history from the University of Barcelona, in museography, design, and shopfitting from the Universitat Politècnica de Catalunya, and in preventive conservation from the Universitat Autònoma de Catalunya. Following family tradition, she entered the antiques field, specializing in Catalan furniture and medieval furnishings in general, in addition to medieval decorative arts. She has worked in Catalan museums and cultural institutions, where she has documented collections of furnishings and decorative arts, managed artistic heritage collections, and coordinated exhibitions. Eva Pascual i Miró has written numerous articles on Catalan decorative arts and medieval furnishings, and taught courses on the history, documentation, and criteria of furniture restoration. She is a regular contributor to specialist magazines.

# The model

Before studying the materials and tools needed to create an architectural model, and the processes this involves, it is important to be aware of the different types of models and the elements that make them up, and to understand the true meaning of the term. Analyzing the concept of an architectural model allows us to establish how it is defined and how it differs from the concept of a model in general, so that we can appreciate the characteristics of both.

Architectural models have a dual function: they are a representation of an object or architectural structure (as in our case) at a reduced scale; but they are also an object in their own right, full of expressive meaning. They have become a first-class means of communication, as they offer a global understanding of architecture, even for those who know nothing about this discipline. They make it possible to understand the spatial relationships, volumes, colors, textures, and finishes of architectural work that is either in a distant location, rendering it impossible to observe directly, or that does not exist, either because it is for a future project or because it has been destroyed.

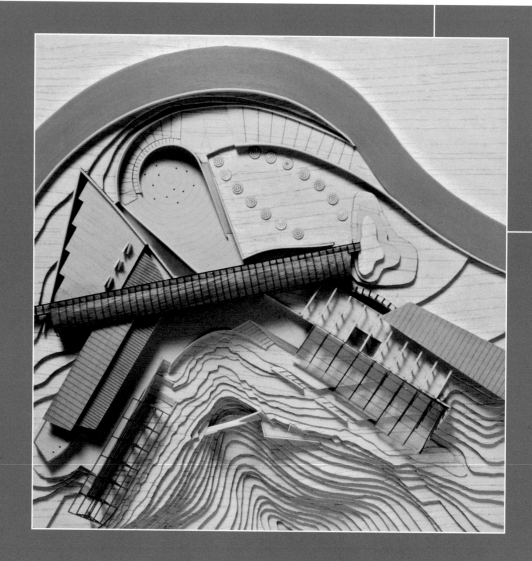

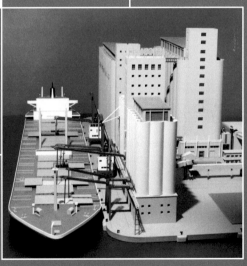

# Architectural models

▲ Tàpies Foundation in Barcelona, Lluís Domènech and Roser Amador, architects. Architectural model of wood and acrylic made by Maquet-barna (scale 1:100), 1984. Architectural model of the interior of the exhibition spaces represented in section. Preexisting architecture is represented here, as well as the distribution and form of the exhibition furniture and seating.

Another term often used for a scale model of an architectural work is the word *maquette*, from the French, which in turn comes from the Italian *macchietta*, the diminutive of *macchia*, which means "sketch" and also "spot." Further back, the Italian derives from the Latin *macula*, from *maculare*, meaning "to spot." Other terms are "architectural scale models," or "3D architectural models." The phrase "architectural model" will be used throughout this book, although often abbreviated to "model" for simplicity.

## Architectural models and models

The concept of an **architectural model** is linked to that of a model, and on occasions the two are confused. In classical Greek, two words were used to refer to an architectural model: *typos* referred to the "type," in other words, to a model or symbol that represented something, for example, an architectural model of a building at a reduced scale; while *paradigm* from the Greek *parádeigma* referred to the pattern or copy of the architectural model at actual size. Therefore, the limits between both concepts, architectural model and model, are somewhat vague. This book concentrates solely on the creation of architectural models.

► Hotel Urban in Madrid, Carles Bassò, architect. Architectural model of acrylic made by Maquet-barna (scale 1:100), 2005. Presentation model of the building showing the production of the façades and enclosures.

A **model** is understood as the copy or original archetype that is used as a kind of pattern, sample, or example to make something by imitating it or reproducing it. Here, a model is considered as the object (also the idea) that is the starting point for a work, as if it were a diagram, and which may undergo changes and adopt final solutions during the creative process that move far from the initial ideas. A model may have the same size as the object it is representing. An architectural model, on the other hand, is a three-dimensional representation of an object or building at a reduced scale: a building, a monument, an ornament, and so on. Its meaning is somewhat closer to simulation and representation. Nevertheless, architectural models provide a foretaste of the work in architectural projects, taking a step toward forming a constructive proposal. Thus the idea here is closer to that of a model. In this case, an architectural model constitutes an intermediate phase in the process, halfway between the initial idea and the final construction. It therefore plays an important role in developing a project. It is an essential instrument in presenting and communicating designs, but also in assessing and checking out solutions that have been proposed, as it allows the structural organization and the spatial and massing composition of the work to be reproduced, as well as showing details of the construction: materials, colors, textures, interrelationship with the environment, and so forth.

Several aspects come together in architectural models: they are an object of study during the development phases of a project; an instrument of communication, in the way that they represent the architecture; and objects in their own right with respect to the architecture they represent, with their own expressive, aesthetic, and artistic value. Given that an architectural model is a manufactured representation of architecture, as an element of communication it makes the interpretation, in itself complex, of a building or its parts (interiors, decorations, structures, etc.) easy and quick. As an object, it allows the architecture to be viewed from different angles and viewpoints than the traditional ones, as the result of the direct observation of any building, and even from unreal viewpoints to explain or demonstrate certain elements. To this should be added the possibilities for personal exploration that it offers observers, who can see the project from different angles, bringing added interest to the object.

▶ Communications tower at the Montjuïc Olympic Ring complex, in Barcelona. Architectural model of acrylic made by Maquet-barna (scale 1:500), after 1992.

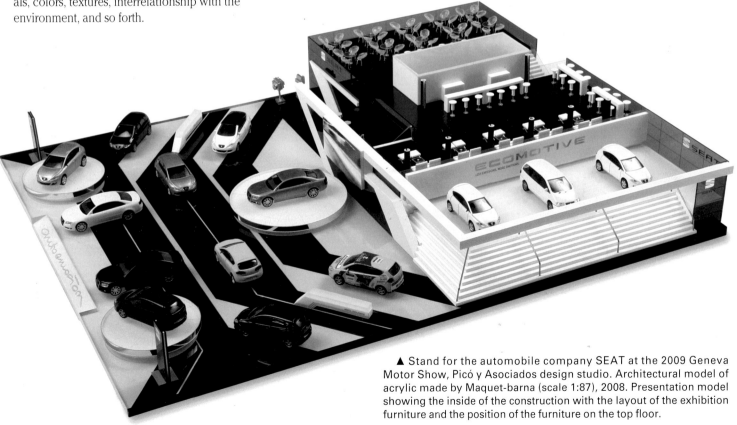

▲ Stand for the automobile company SEAT at the 2009 Geneva Motor Show, Picó y Asociados design studio. Architectural model of acrylic made by Maquet-barna (scale 1:87), 2008. Presentation model showing the inside of the construction with the layout of the exhibition furniture and the position of the furniture on the top floor.

# Types of architectural models

Architectural models are classified into different types according to the phase of the architectural project that they cover, depending on what they represent, the reason why they were created, or the basic elements involved in making them. However, in most cases, they are a combination of elements and types, meaning that they can be classified into several types.

## Types according to the phases of a project

### Working models and presentation models

Architectural projects often require the creation of working models. These are made in the architecture studio and are used as a starting point to work on the architectural idea or to specify details; they can therefore be considered as a testing ground by which it is possible to clarify or rule out various concepts, giving shape to them in a three-dimensional representation. These architectural models, considered to be for the purposes of experimentation or a first draft, are made with low-cost materials that are easy to source and to work with using common tools, as they need to allow as many modifications and changes as necessary in terms of form, material, or scale. They have varying degrees of definition depending on the needs of each project and on the architect, and in some cases they are no more than mere conceptual sketches. Even so, they should represent the contents of the project artificially, offering the chance to rapidly visualize the nature of the work to be done. As an integral part of the processes involved in defining a project, these architectural models are included within the phases and work involved in architecture itself. The study of this kind of architectural model goes beyond the physical limits of this book, being more suited to books on architectural practice.

**Presentation models** provide a representation of the final appearance of a design. Usually created in a specialist workshop using durable, resistant, and high quality materials, with meticulous finishes, they are made with a high degree of definition to offer an illustrative image, which means that everybody can understand the architecture they represent. Compared to the working models, changes are not made to these models, and they can have a wealth of detail in the finishes, colors, textures, accessories, and so on, to realistically suggest the architecture and its surroundings, if this is relevant. They are used for exhibition and for demonstration purposes, as well as in competitions. In the first two cases, they are generally extremely detailed and can be accompanied by naturalistic representations and finishes. For competitions, relatively detailed models are made with special or innovative materials, designed to create interesting effects. Although it is most common to make working models during the draft and basic design phases, presentation models can also be made to illustrate any phase of architectural practice, as will be explained below.

### The draft phase

The building's key aspects and general characteristics are displayed in the draft phase. Presentation models offer an initial global picture of the architecture and general forms of a building; they do not usually contain excessive detail, and they use massing values to achieve an illustrative image.

▲ ▶ Sports stadium in Abu Dhabi, Joaquim Pujol, architect. Architectural model of wood made by Maquet-barna (scale 1:500), 2004. Two views of the presentation model in which the general forms of the building are shown using massing elements.

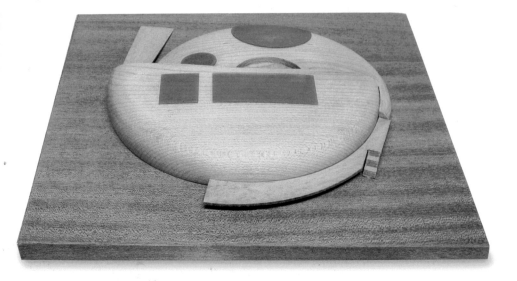

## The design phase

The general characteristics of the architecture are precisely defined during the design or basic design phase through the adoption of specific solutions. The architectural models here are at a more advanced stage than those of the draft phase, with all the solutions and forms that are to characterize the building.

▶ Highway service station, GCA Arquitectes Associats. Architectural model of acrylic made by Maquet-barna (scale 1:200), 2002. The model, made for a competition, reflects the specific forms of the design and the way that solutions of space, enclosures, supports, and circulation have been dealt with.

## The implementation phase

The initial design phase takes shape during what is known as the implementation phase, where all of the details and specific characteristics of the building are conclusively determined, including materials, colors, special elements, equipment, and building systems. The architectural models illustrate the building exactly as it will be once completed, paying attention to details and finishes.

◀ Highway service station, Picó y Asociados design studio. Architectural model of acrylic made by Maquet-barna (scale 1:200), 2002. All details are shown in implementation models, with special attention to the finishes.

▶ Detail of the previous model in which the building's circular floor plan can be seen. The characteristics of the glass walls and the supports are shown, as well as the design of the roof and the organization of the interior space and the location of the furniture.

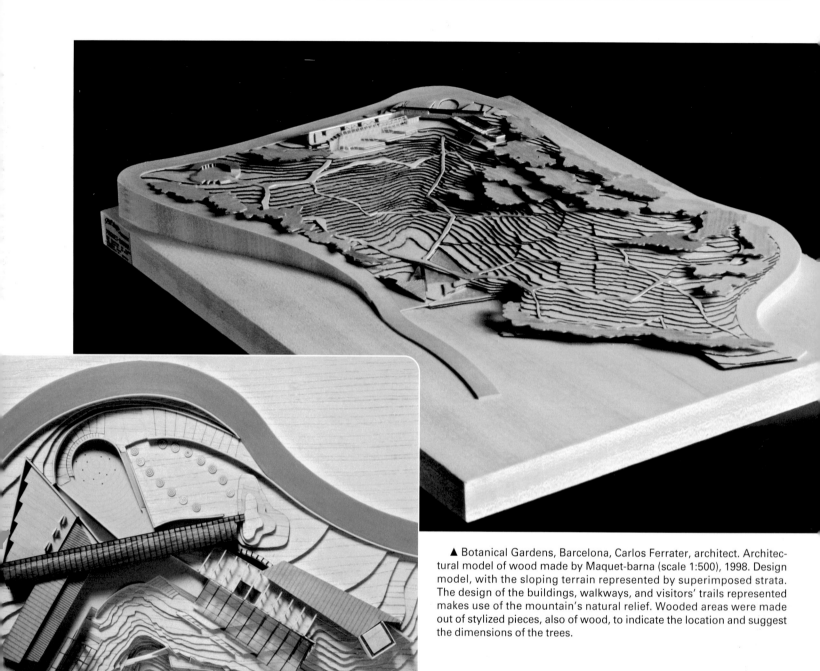

▲ Botanical Gardens, Barcelona, Carlos Ferrater, architect. Architectural model of wood made by Maquet-barna (scale 1:500), 1998. Design model, with the sloping terrain represented by superimposed strata. The design of the buildings, walkways, and visitors' trails represented makes use of the mountain's natural relief. Wooded areas were made out of stylized pieces, also of wood, to indicate the location and suggest the dimensions of the trees.

◄ Detail of architectural model of the Botanical Gardens buildings. The buildings represented in this model show their relationship with the surroundings, characterized by steeply sloping terrain.

# Types according to what they represent

**Topographic models** reproduce the surface of an existing plot of land in a relatively detailed manner, depending on the phase of the project, the scale, and the purpose of each model. They may represent terrain or a natural landscape, as well as any work that is to be done on it, and also urban elements like parks, gardens, and playing fields. These architectural models represent the surface, vegetation, and relief, and often contain elements that contribute to giving an idea of the scale used, such as street furniture, people, and transport systems.

**Terrain models** represent the configuration of a surface and all of its features, showing the topography and forms of relief, along with their specific characteristics. They are often the base onto which the buildings are placed. They may also show built surface areas, roads, vegetation or groups of trees, and water areas. Topography is typically represented by strata that are based on the contour lines of a ground plan, at the scale at which the architectural model is to be made.

▶ Landscaping in an orchard, Albert Pedrero, architecture student. Architectural model of foam board and acrylic made by Maquet-barna (scale 1:200), 2003. Landscape model of an orchard adjoining a home, showing the position of the buildings and the swimming pool in relation to the existing trees.

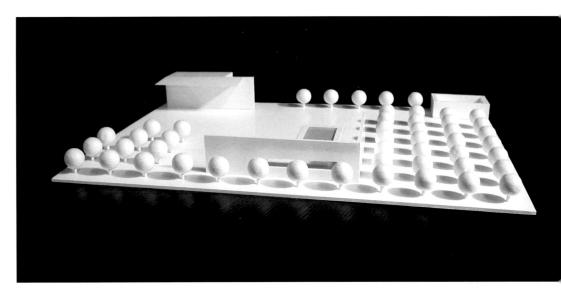

**Landscape models** represent the forms of a geographical space in which the inherent natural elements of the land interrelate with others that are the result of human intervention, working in unison. The forms of the ground and the spaces of the landscape are represented in these architectural models, with areas of vegetation shown alongside areas of circulation, buildings, and furniture, if relevant. Many resources are available to represent plant elements, from materials with a very naturalistic appearance to others that are more abstract, suggesting vegetation in a simple and schematic, almost conceptual, manner, through volumes or forms, and usually focusing on trees.

In **natural landscape models**, representations can be more naturalistic, and reproduce the characteristics of the terrain, vegetation, and water in a descriptive way.

**Garden models** are the partial representation of a landscape or plot of land planned by people in which plant species with ornamental purposes are grown. These represent elements specific to gardens (such as ponds and water areas, fences and railings, plants, flowerbeds and lawn areas, paths and tracks, rockeries, arboretums and orchards) and buildings (such as cabins, arbors, pergolas, conservatories, and pavilions). These architectural models can portray a wide variety of spaces—squares, pedestrian areas, terraces, balconies, and hanging gardens; interior courtyards, sports fields, and swimming pools; and botanical, zoological, and historical gardens.

▶ Detail of a historical model of the monastery of Sant Llorenç prop Bagà and its surroundings in the fifteenth century. Architectural model of acrylic and polyurethane foam made by Maquet-barna (scale 1:100), 2008. The landscape is represented naturalistically, simulating the characteristics and relief of the site along with existing vegetation. The buildings (mills), ponds, and the system of waterways that pow-ered the mills are also represented.

## Building models

Building models focus on showing the characteristics of a building; they might be urban planning, building, structural, interior, or detail models.

**Urban planning models** show the building within the context of its environment, indicating how it is organized and laid out, and establishing contextual relationships, both as concerns the terrain represented with its topographic characteristics and the other existing buildings, depending on circumstances. They may show a single building or project in a very large area that includes numerous structures, in all cases reflecting the size and proportions of the buildings within the context of their environment. Preexisting buildings are usually represented using massing elements. They can also show circulation flows in the vicinity, as well as the way the spaces are laid out, delimited, and used.

**Building models** show the spatial and constructive characteristics of the building and its shapes, with or without depicting the environment. In general, the most important enclosures of the building, like façades and roofs, can be seen. However, a building can be represented in other ways; for example, it may have a transparent or removable façade or roof that allows the interior to be shown.

**Structural models** are used to show the specific uses and characteristics of the construction without representing the building as a whole.

**Interior models** show the interior space of a building, either totally or partially. They are used to establish spatial, circulation, and organizational relationships, as well as lighting options. They represent in detail the furniture, materials, and colors of the interior, sometimes using human figures to give an idea of the proportions. Different resources are available to show interiors: for example, the roof may be left off so that the ground plan can be seen, a sectional model created to give a vertical view, or strategically positioned openings made. These architectural models, showing a vertical section of the building, mean that the organization and relationships of space on the different floors can be made visible.

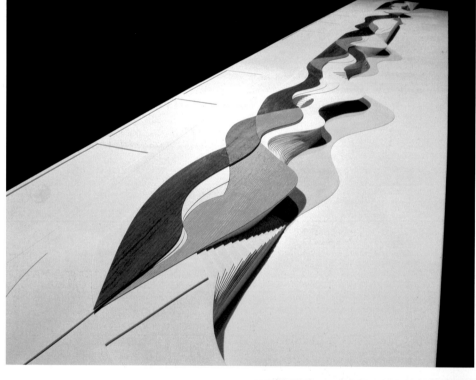

◀ Esplanade of a beach, the Playa de Poniente, in Benidorm, Alicante, Carlos Ferrater, architect. Architectural model of acrylic and wood made by Maquet-barna (scale 1:500), 2002. Example of an urban planning model showing the layout and organization of an esplanade, thought out as an intermediate space between the city and the natural space of the beach. The topography and shapes that make up the border with the beach have been represented topographically using strata, while the different types of wood represent the textures of the paving at the top and the beach at the bottom. Access points to the beach are also shown.

▶ Project for the port of Mataró, Alonso, Balaguer y Arquitectos Asociados. Architectural model of acrylic made by Maquet-barna (scale 1:500), 2003. Urban planning model showing the organization of a large area that includes the construction of buildings and layout of the surroundings. The projected buildings were made with strata of clear acrylic, suggesting the floors of each, while existing buildings were produced in white acrylic. Other areas of design and layout of the surroundings used colors that suggested their purpose, and the plant elements were made of foam.

▲ The Gran Teatre del Liceu in Barcelona, Ignasi de Solà-Morales, Lluís Dilmé, and Xavier Fabré, architects. Architectural model of wood and metal made by Maquet-barna (scale 1:100), 1997. Building model showing the original building and the new extension to the theater, representing the façades and roofs.

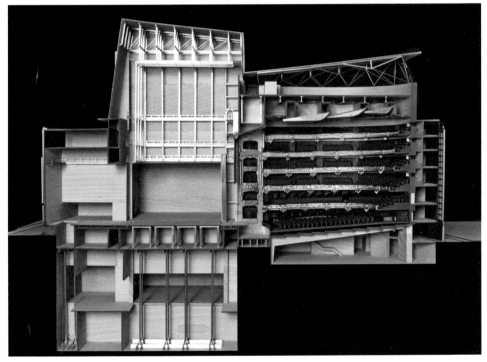

◀ Interior section of the Gran Teatre del Liceu which shows the auditorium and the stage. Made of wood by Maquet-barna (scale 1:100), 1997. The interior of the auditorium is represented in great detail, showing the distribution across the various floors and including ornamental elements, lighting, and furniture; the colors are also emphasized. The model also shows the structure of the building and the roof. On the stage, the structure and systems used for scene changes are visible.

Finally, **detail models** are useful when we wish to represent certain elements of a building that must be shown in great detail due to their special characteristics or complexity. These may be construction elements (joins, beams, roofs, windows, rails, etc.) or decorative details, for example, of a façade or furniture. Such models demonstrate the shapes and material values of each element in considerable detail.

▶ Terminal 1 of Barcelona Airport, Ricardo Bofill, architect. Architectural model of acrylic made by Maquet-barna (scale 1:400), 2003. Sectional model, which shows the structure of the roof and the enclosures, as well as the layout of the interior space.

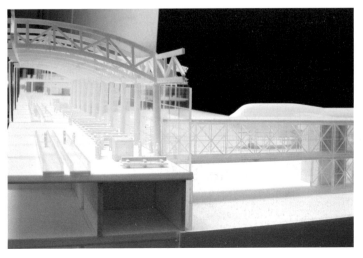

# Types according to purpose

### Exhibition models

Exhibition models are useful for the purpose of illustration, as they represent the general appearance of the work, communicating and transmitting the essential values of a project. The best known are architectural models commissioned by property developers for the sale of real estate, as well as those that are made for public works, to present a project to the inhabitants of a town or city, or to enter into a competition. Nevertheless, exhibition or illustrative models are also used to show other kinds of buildings such as factories or telecommunications and energy installations, as well as to illustrate specific aspects that are hard to express in other ways, like certain industrial processes or complex flow patterns in public buildings.

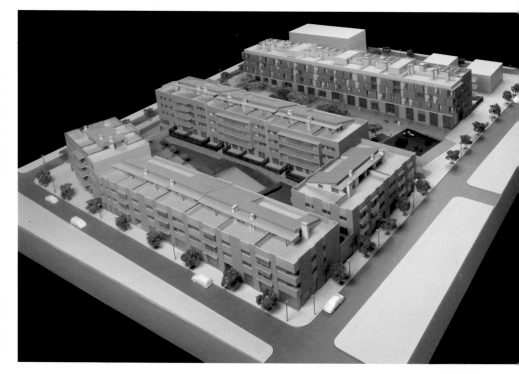

► Development of 190 homes in Llinars del Vallès, Manolo Ortiz Alba, architect (Oiskosvia architecture, s.c.c.l.), developer Llinars Residencial, S.A. (Grup l'Ull Blau). Architectural model of acrylic made by Maquet-barna (scale 1:100), 2009. Illustrative model aimed at potential buyers showing the characteristics of the buildings and the design of the surrounding area.

▼ Silos and loading bay for the company Ergransa, in Barcelona. Architectural model of acrylic made by Maquet-barna (scale 1:100), 1982. Illustrative model of storage facilities in the port of Barcelona.

▲ Proposed project for the port of Las Palmas de Gran Canaria, Carlos Ferrater, architect. Architectural model of acrylic made by Maquet-barna (scale 1:1,000), 2005. Detail of the model for the planning competition of the port area of Las Palmas, covering a total area of 323,000 sq ft (30,000 m²). It shows a public planning project which involved the construction of new buildings, as well as the layout of the surroundings and the seafront. Some of the new buildings have been represented by massing elements of translucent acrylic lit at the bottom, while the two buildings located within the port are represented with sheets of acrylic, also lit to suggest their volumes.

▶ Old Río Tinto explosives factory, in Tarragona. Architectural model of acrylic made by Maquet-barna (scale 1:200), 1980. Illustrative model of an industrial facility.

◀▼ Project to install a photovoltaic noise barrier—DV SoundPeu in Freising, Germany, Isofotón S.A. Architectural model of acrylic made by Maquet-barna (scale 1:500), 2003. Exhibition model of a project to install photovoltaic modules as a sound barrier to insulate homes from highway noise and produce energy. It shows the project design as well as the architectural model of one module, the latter to a scale of 1:100.

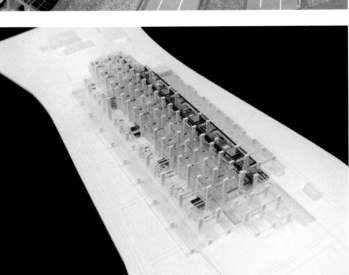

◀ Interior circulation in Toledo Hospital, Carlos Ferrater, architect. Architectural model of acrylic made by Maquet-barna (scale 1:400), 2002. Architectural model of the ground plan of the hospital interior. It shows the structure of the building, and the circulation routes or flows of patients are marked in different colors.

## Demonstration models

Demonstration models are used to document concepts that would be difficult to grasp if presented in any other way, allowing viewers to understand the project quickly and easily. They represent the general appearance of the project in great detail. They are exhibited in museums, exhibitions, interpretation or information centers, archeological sites, nature centers, and so on. The most common are models of historical and archeological representations, although there are also models of military battles and campaigns, machines, and work systems, among other things. Models made especially for people with sensory disabilities are also available.

▼ Hospital de la Santa Creu i Sant Pau, Lluís Domènech i Muntaner, architect (1902–1930). Architectural model of acrylic and wood made by Maquet-barna (scale 1:200), 1996. This architectural model of the collection of buildings that make up the hospital was created for a permanent exhibition at the Museu d'Història de Catalunya in Barcelona. It is used as a resource to document one of the most symbolic sites in Catalan Modernist architecture, declared a UNESCO World Heritage Site in 1997.

▼ Iberian settlement at Turó de Montgrós in El Brull (Barcelona). Architectural model of acrylic and polyurethane foam made by Maquet-barna (scale 1:100), 2008. Historical model of the reconstruction of an Iberian settlement occupied from 1000 BC and discovered in 1975. It uses a naturalistic style to show the site and the buildings. The model is on display in the information center that accompanies the archeological site.

▲ La Seu Vella in Lleida (ancient Ilerda). Architectural model of wood made by Maquet-barna (scale 1:100), 1990. Architectural model of the old cathedral in Lleida (completed in the fifteenth century) represented in longitudinal section, so that people with visual disability can appreciate the structure and decoration of the building.

▼ ► Centcelles Mausoleum, in Tarragona. Architectural model of wood made by Maquet-barna (scale 1:100), 1990. Architectural model of a Roman mausoleum made for the visually impaired. A practicable model was created which, when opened, presented the longitudinal section of the building showing its structure and massing.

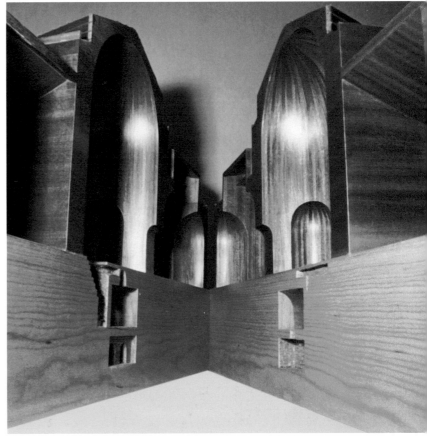

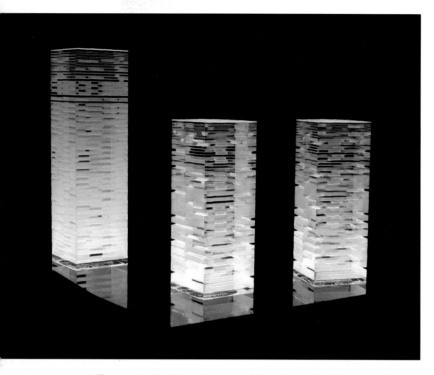

▲ Towers in the Plaza Europa in L'Hospitalet de Llobregat, Alonso, Balaguer y Arquitectos Asociados. Architectural model of acrylic made by Maquet-barna (scale 1:400), 2004. Massing model of the towers made in blocks of laser-cut acrylic to suggest the floors of the buildings and underlit.

# Types according to elements used

Types of architectural models can also be defined based on the basic elements used to make them. It is possible to employ masses, rods, or planes to create massing, structural, or surface models, although most architectural models are, in fact, a combination of these elements, and in practice it is possible to use any of them to create any model.

### Massing models

Massing models are made from blocks that represent the buildings. The general form of the building and its volume is shown here, as well as its relationship with its environment, whether land or other buildings.

▼ Espai Subirachs, Ramon Sanabria and Lidia Planas, architects. Architectural model of acrylic made by Maquet-barna (scale 1:100), 2003. Sectional model in which the interior mass of the building can be seen. The prominence of the covered central courtyard (an empty space) can be observed in contrast to the two masses of the building that make up the exhibition halls and other rooms in the institution. The building's relationship to the masses of the surrounding structures can also be seen, as well as its façades and roofs.

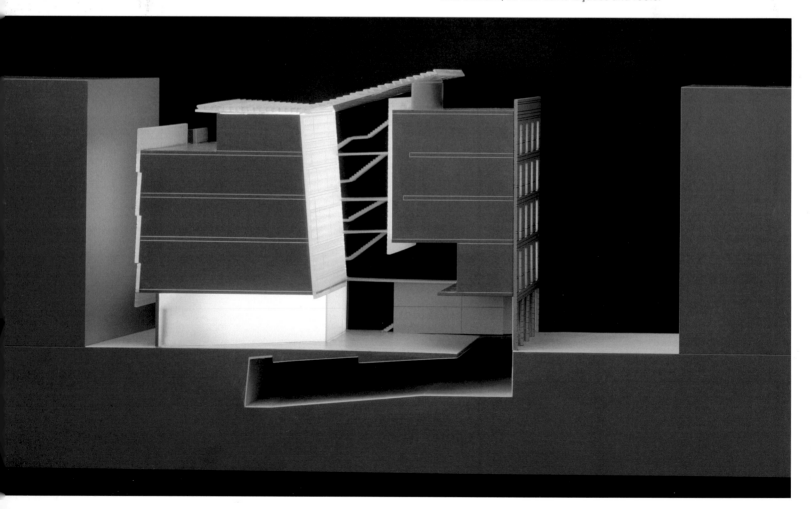

## Structural models

Rods and lines are used to create structural models or detailed models to represent a building's roofs, supports, or enclosures, for example, as well as bridges or footbridges.

## Surface models

Surface areas and planes are used to create architectural models of buildings in which planes like façades, roofs, and enclosures prevail, as in specific models of façades, interior sections, and so on.

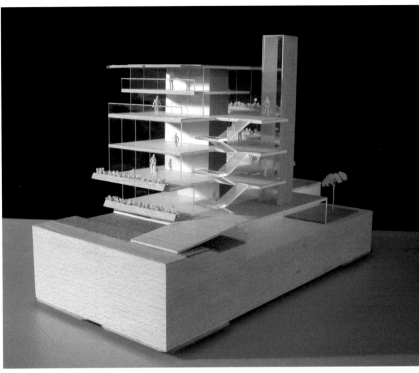

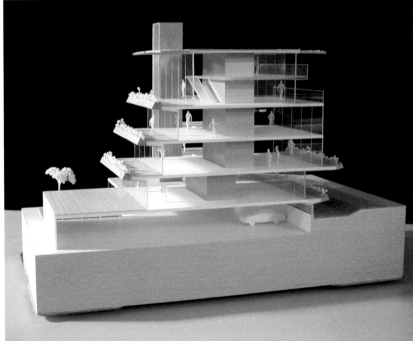

▲ ▲ Apartment building in La Moraleja, Madrid, Alonso, Balaguer y Arquitectos Asociados. Architectural model of acrylic and wood made by Maquet-barna (scale 1:100), 2005. General and spatial structural model of a building, in which planes were used as elements in its construction.

◀ Seat of the government of Cantabria in Santander, Carlos Ferrater, architect. Architectural model of acrylic made by Maquet-barna (scale 1:200), 2001. Detail of the façades and the roofs.

This section describes the main materials and tools used to make architectural models. They have been grouped in such a way that the reader can easily find everything that is needed to carry out each technical process. You will also find a description of each tool, an explanation of its possible uses, and, when required, safety advice. This section includes specific instructions on organization and safety in the workshop—a vital aspect when working on architectural models.

Architectural modelmaking involves multiple processes that require detailed knowledge of materials and of a wide range of tools. Given that it is possible to use an almost infinite variety of materials, it is essential that we understand their characteristics in advance in order to do our work successfully. Moreover, this information will be the starting point for technical innovation.

# Materials and tools

# Basic materials

## Paper, paperboard, and cardboard

Paper is a sheet obtained from binding fibers of plant origin (made up of a certain proportion of cellulose) that has been previously treated and refined, along with other added materials like glues, fillers, and pigments. The fibers are superimposed one on the other and are pressed in a similar fashion to felt. There are different types of paper depending on composition, finishes, and weight. In the United States the weight of the paper is determined based on the weight of a ream (500 sheets) of a given size; in the rest of the world paper weight is measured in reference to a surface measurement; in general, grams per square meter. A high-weight paper weighs more and is thicker than one with lower weight. The weight of paper is usually lower than 150-pound (180–200 g/m$^2$); paper for everyday use is between 50- and 80-pound (80 and 90 g/m$^2$). Paperboard is thick paper commonly sold in the United States by point size, for example, 70-, 80-, 90-, and 100-pt (in metric terms, it has a grammage higher than 180–200 g/m$^2$ and up to 350 g/m$^2$); cardboard is even heavier and is sold by thickness.

Many types of paper, paperboard, and cardboard can be used to create architectural models. They range from everyday versions to special or coated versions that have an outer layer that may be colored, shiny, satin, or matte, or have a metallic look. They can also have a corrugated surface with regular grooves or ridges.

These materials are mainly used to make working models, as they are cheap, easy to source and to work with, and allow any changes to be made quickly and easily.

▶ Paper

▲ Special paper

▶ Cardboard

◄ Corrugated cardboard in different thicknesses with coatings in black, gray, and silver

▼ White foam board

## Foam board

Foam board, or foamcore, is made of a central sheet of polyurethane foam placed between two strips of paperboard. The result is a very light and rigid material that can be folded without breaking and can be cut easily with a utility knife or scalpel. Holes can be made in it, and it can be painted and decorated. It is sold in sheets of different thicknesses, although the most common are ⅛, ³⁄₁₆, and ½ in (3, 5, 10, and 15 mm) thick; this varies depending on the manufacturer. The central foam is usually white, but sheets are also made in black foam.

Sheets of foam board can be bought in whites, grays or blacks, and colors may even be combined on the same sheet, with each side in one color. Foam board is also available with self-adhesive strips on one or both sides and aluminum reinforcement, among other things. It is mainly used to make working models, and on occasion, presentation models.

## Cork

Cork is a plant tissue made up of cells in which the cellulose of the membrane has turned into suberin (an impermeable and elastic substance). It is mainly found in the trunk of the cork tree in the form of thin strips, although it can be several inches thick in some species. Industrial cork is a product extracted from the bark of the cork oak. It is very thick, light, and impermeable, with insulating qualities. It is cleaned, ground, bound, and pressed, producing blocks of agglomerate that are cut and sold in sheets and rolls, in different forms and even in granules. Cork is useful for making project and presentation models, and is ideal for large-dimension topographic models.

► Cork

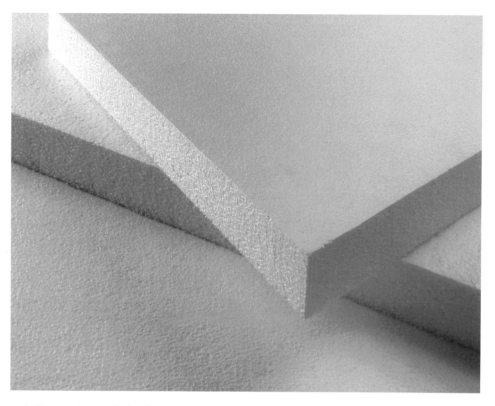

▲ Sheets of expanded polystyrene

## Expanded polystyrene

Expanded polystyrene (EPS) is a thermo-plastic polymer that can be molded easily due to a blowing agent (a gas that reduces the density of the material), so that the resulting product is made up of 98 percent air and 2 percent polystyrene. It is a very light, low-density material. It has thermal and acoustic insulating qualities, and is resistant to humidity and impacts; it is therefore used as an insulator in construction and for packing fragile and fresh products. The name "Styrofoam" is often used as a generic term for EPS. It can be bought in sheets or in blocks, with a density that varies according to the manufacturer. It is also possible to buy ready-cut pieces in different shapes. EPS is a cheap material that is easy to source and to work with, although it has to be cut with a special thermal cutter. It is very suitable for creating massing models.

# Gypsum

Gypsum is a calcium sulphate dihydrate with the formula $CaSO_4 \cdot 2H_2O$. It is found in nature in the form of colorless crystals that can be exfoliated in sheets. It has low hardness, and is soft and pliant. It is sold in a dehydrated form as a white powder, and hardens once mixed with water. Gypsum is used a great deal because of its characteristics—strength, setting time—and its closely controlled qualities of expansion and contraction. This material has traditionally been the most popular choice for presentation models, and above all for representing heritage architecture to a large scale; on occasion, techniques similar to those used in sculpture are employed depending on the model, although these days other machinable materials that save time and give a stronger result are often substituted.

◄ Gypsum and water

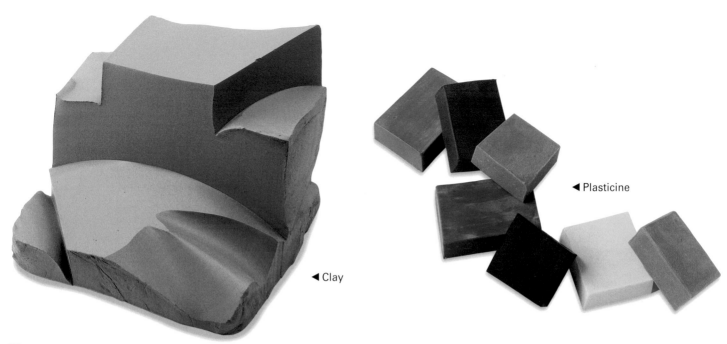

◄ Plasticine

◄ Clay

## Clay

Clay is the result of the decomposition of feldspathic rocks (very abundant in the earth's crust) due to the action of water over millions of years. It is a hydrated aluminum silicate, made up of approximately 40 percent aluminum (aluminum oxide), 40 percent silica (silicon oxide), and 14 percent water. Given that clay is a pliant material, once molded it maintains the form it has been given, and shrinks or recedes during drying and firing. Through modelling, it can be used to create working models, although its main inconvenience is the reduction of volume (shrinkage) during drying.

## Plasticine

Plasticine is a malleable material made up mainly of calcium salts, petroleum jelly, and stearic acid, although the composition varies depending on the manufacturer. It is sold in a wide variety of colors, and is cheap and easy to source. It is easily molded, which makes it ideal for use in school craft projects. In architectural modelmaking, it is useful for creating working models.

## Polyurethane foam

Polyurethane foam is a foamed thermo-plastic synthetic resin that is made by the mixing and reaction of two basic components: isocyanate and polyol (an alcohol), along with other components and additives. The chemical reaction caused by mixing releases carbon dioxide, which produces the

▲ Sheets and blocks of polyurethane foam

bubbles that make up the foam. This is a very strong, porous material, with a solid and uniform structure, and it is a good insulator that is resistant to acids, water, and humidity. It is used as an upholstery filling, and as an insulator in construction and the automotive industry, among other things. Independently of its density, the foam can be flexible, semi-rigid, or rigid; therefore, it can be low density and firm (as for mattresses and furniture) or high density and soft. The surface of the foam is characterized by its firmness and the support offered, in other words, by its resistance to deformation. In architectural modelmak-

ing it is used to create volumes in presentation models, being particularly well suited for curved surfaces because it is easy to cut and shape, as well as for making stands for topographic models, because it is very strong while also very light. The type of foam chosen has to depend on the use to which it is to be put.

# Wood

A great variety of types of wood can be used to create presentation models. Wood comes in planks, solid form, veneers, or in battens with different shapes and forms. The most commonly used are made of balsa and birch.

### Balsa

Balsa (*Ochroma lagopus*) is a soft, very light, elastic, and low-density wood, with a straight and regular grain. Its color ranges from lustrous pinkish-beige to pale straw. It has a smooth texture and is velvety to the touch. It is very porous, with a continuous grain, and is not very stable. In general, it is sold in sheets, blocks, or strips as narrow as 4 in x 36 in (100 x 1,000 mm) and from $\frac{1}{32}$ in to 3 in (1, 1.5, 2, 2.5 or 3 to 10 mm) thick.

### Birch

Birch (*Betula pendula, Betula alba, Betula verrucosa*) is a strong, medium-density hardwood. Its color ranges from white to yellowish, pink, and reddish, with short and

▲ Balsa

▲ Birch

compact veins. Exceptionally, it presents brightly colored veins and occasional dark blotches. It has a firm and uniform texture. Birch does not crack or corrode, although it can rot due to excess humidity. For architectural modelmaking, birch is usually sold in plywood sheets in a wide range of fractions of an inch (0.6, 1, 2, 3, and 5 mm) thick.

### Veneers

Veneers are very thin sheets of wood between $\frac{1}{64}$ and $\frac{1}{8}$ in (0.2 and 5 mm) thick. The appearance and grain of veneers depend on the part of the tree from which the wood is taken and the way it is cut. Veneers can have different types of grain effects: smooth with a regular grain, a rippled grain, a water effect with sinuous waves, speckled with closely spaced small knots, knotty, gnarled with irregular patterns and accentuated coloration, sinuous grain, and more. There are also veneers available that have been made of blockboard with a very straight and marked grain, as well as a variety of dyed veneers in a range of colors. In architectural modelmaking, veneers are usually used to cover other surfaces. They are placed on top of the model's base material in order to decorate the surface or to create certain effects or details.

◄ Various dyed blockboard veneers

### Plywood

Plywood is made up of panels of wood glued crosswise over each other according to the fibers of each panel. The panels are glued in alternately, with the direction of the fiber or the grain of alternate sheets at right angles. This produces a stable board that is resistant to warping. Plywood is classified into three categories depending on the quality of the face side. Class A includes plywood with faces that have an even appearance, without imperfections. Class B includes plywood with some imperfections, for example, small knots or blotches. Those which have large knots and even cracks are in Class C. Plywood panel measurements vary from a thickness of ⅛ to 1 in (3 to 30 mm), a length of 8 to 12 ft (2.44 to 3.66 m) and a width of 4 to 8 ft (1.22 to 1.52 m). In architectural modelmaking, plywood is used to make the bases or stands.

### Chipboard

Chipboard, also known as particle board, is made by gluing together sawdust with synthetic resins under pressure at a high temperature. Different types of chipboard are manufactured, depending on the shape and size of the wood particles, their distribution, and the type of resins used as an adhesive. Chipboard is more stable than plywood and

does not have the typical defects of solid wood. It is used to make bases or stands for architectural models.

### Fiberboard

Fiberboard is made up of wood that has been broken down into fibers bound together by synthetic resins in a high-frequency press that yields a reconstituted wood. Boards are manufactured in different densities depending on the amount of pressure used and the type of resins: high-density (HDF), low-density (LDF), and medium-density (MDF). The latter is made by binding dry wood fibers with synthetic resins; the result is a fine-textured, uniform structure that gives the faces and edges a perfect finish. It is used and worked as a wood substitute. MDF is made in thicknesses that range between ¼ and ½ in (6 and 32 mm), but the most common board size is 4 feet (1.2 m) wide by 8 ft (2.4 m) high. Fiberboard is used in a similar way to the board types mentioned above.

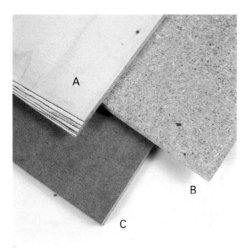

▲ Plywood (A), chipboard (B), and medium-density fiberboard (MDF) (C)

▶ Sapele (A), birch (B), and beech (C) veneers; water-effect veneer (D) and dyed veneer (E)

# Metal

Brass is an alloy of copper (Cu) and zinc (Zn) (5 to 45% zinc) with other metals: aluminum (Al), lead (Pb), tin (Sn), manganese (Mn), or silicon (Si), among others. The composition of the alloy and the percentage of zinc determine the mechanical characteristics, fusibility, and capacity of the metal during smelting or forging, as well as the stamping and machining of each type of brass. Harder than copper, brass is ductile and easy to machine, engrave, and melt. Its malleability varies according to its composition. With a pale yellow color, it can be polished to achieve a high golden sheen. It is sold in solid sheets, corrugated sheets, expanded sheets, and in grilles, with diagonal, round, square, octagonal, or romboidal holes. It is also found in assorted profiles (in the forms of H, T, I, L, U, or C, in different sizes), in round bars, square bars and in square and round tubes, all in a wide variety of sizes. Brass is useful always for creating presentation models.

◄ Various brass profiles, bars, and tubes

▼ Sheets of brass (A), aluminum (B), and stainless steel (C), expanded brass (D), expanded aluminum (E), and expanded and corrugated aluminum (F)

### Aluminum

Aluminum (Al) is a silver-gray metal with a slightly bluish tinge. It is light and soft but strong, very malleable, and ductile. It is especially suitable for smelting and machining. It is also a very good conductor. In its pure state aluminum is fragile and very soft. It is therefore alloyed with other metals in small amounts: copper (Cu), manganese (Mn), magnesium (Mg), or silicon (Si), as well as with other elements depending on the use required of the material. It is sold in smooth sheets, and also in corrugated sheets, with grooves, either plain or crossed and in different formats, and in expanded sheets. It is also available in round tubes of different diameters and in rectangular and square, square rods. Aluminum is used for the same purposes as brass.

### Stainless steel

Steel is an alloy of iron and carbon in different proportions. It is a strong, hard, ductile, and malleable material. This makes it easy to machine, but it also rusts easily. Stainless steel is an alloy of steel with other metals, mainly chrome (Cr), at a minimum of 10.5 percent, which makes it resistant to rust. Some types of stainless steel also contain nickel (Ni) and molybdenum (Mo). It is sold in sheets and in round tubes in various sizes. Stainless steel is used in similar ways to the metals mentioned above.

## Acrylic

Polymethyl methacrylate (PMMA), commonly known as acrylic, is a plastic made by polymerizing methyl methacrylate. With excellent transparency (it is the most transparent plastic) and optical quality, it is light and very resistant to the elements and ultraviolet rays, as well as to impact (compared to glass), but it is easily scratched. Acrylic is resistant to a large number of chemical compounds, although it is susceptible to some acetates and acetones, acids, and solvents. It is very easy to mold and machine, which means it can be worked by cutting or sawing.

▲ The surfaces of the acrylic sheets are protected with a sheet of polythene to keep the material from being scratched during handling, shipping, or storage.

It can be polished and given a translucent effect. To fold acrylic, it needs to be heated beforehand. It is sold under different commercial names: Plexiglas, Vitroflex, Lucite, Acrylite, Acrylplast, Polycast, Oroglass, Limacryl, among others.

Acrylic comes in sheets, rods, tubes, and shapes (balls and cubes), as well as in a wide variety of colors, finishes, and effects (metallic or translucent), depending on the manufacturer. Special pieces and sheets that are cut according to the specific needs of a project can be ordered. The surface of the sheets is protected by a masking film to prevent the material from being scratched during handling. Due to its somewhat high cost, acrylic is used exclusively for presentation models.

▶ Samples of acrylic. The variety of colors and finishes can be seen.

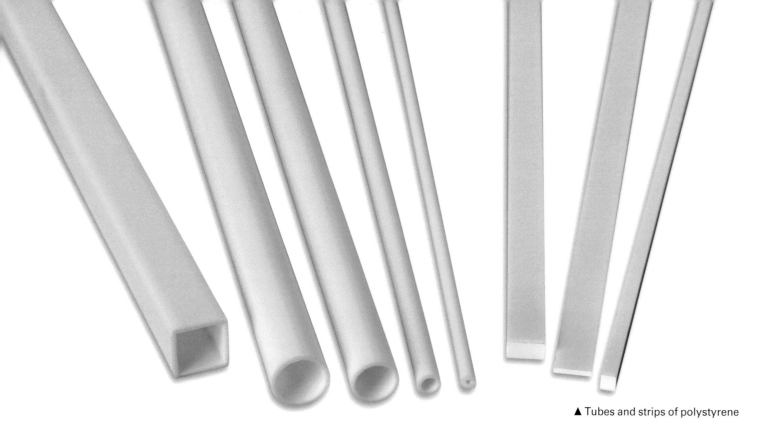

▲ Tubes and strips of polystyrene

## Polystyrene

Polystyrene (PS) is a plastic made by polymerizing styrene. It is cheap, easy to work, and can be painted. Although it is quite fragile, it offers good mechanical resistance to blows. However, it is not resistant to high temperatures, as it deforms easily at less than 212°F (100°C). Pure polystyrene is called crystal polystyrene or general purpose polystyrene; it is a transparent, fragile, and hard plastic, which is shaped or molded at temperatures above 212° F (100° C). It is also possible to create copolymers to improve the material's resistance by adding rubber, which gives high-impact polystyrene (HIPS). This material is opaque, is stronger than pure polystyrene, and offers good resistance to blows. These plastics are mainly used to create objects and containers using different systems (molding, thermoforming, or extrusion). Other varieties are expanded polystyrene (described earlier) and extruded polystyrene, a rigid foam made from crystal polystyrene using gas injection. Both are mainly used as insulators.

Polystyrene is also employed to create different elements of architectural models: sheets that represent floor coverings (brick or granite, in addition to other rubber or veneer-type assemblies), walls (bricks, plasterwork,

▼ Samples of polystyrene sheets used to represent tiled roofs

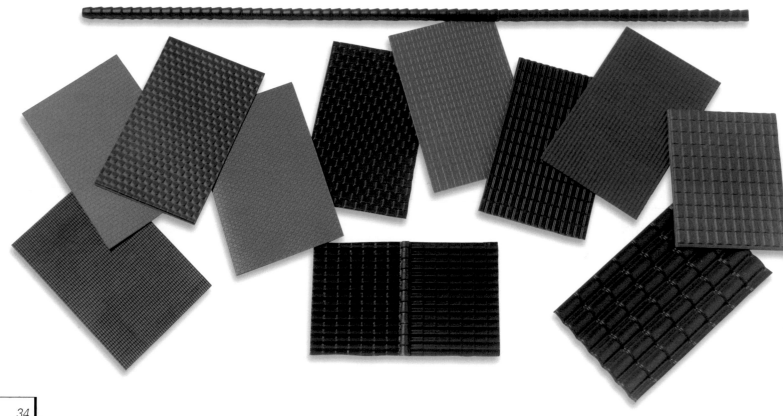

► Tubes and profiles of ABS

stone, or masonry), roofs (tile, slate, or veneer), and pergolas, as well as smooth, engraved, rippled, or corrugated sheets of different sizes. It is also used to make profiles, tubes (square, rectangular, and round), strips, and rods, some with half-round section. These elements are exclusively used in presentation models.

## ABS

Acrylonitrile butadiene styrene, or ABS, is a copolymer made by polymerizing styrene and acrylonitrile in the presence of polybutadiene. It is a hard, rigid, and resilient plastic that is very resistant to blows and abrasion. It can be used in alloys with other plastics. It is used to make car parts, and to produce a large number of objects that need to be light but rigid at the same time, such as casings for electronic apparatus, toys, and so on. ABS is employed to make different elements for architectural modelmaking: smooth sheets from .003 to .125 in (0.5 to 3.2 mm) thick, profiles, and tubes.

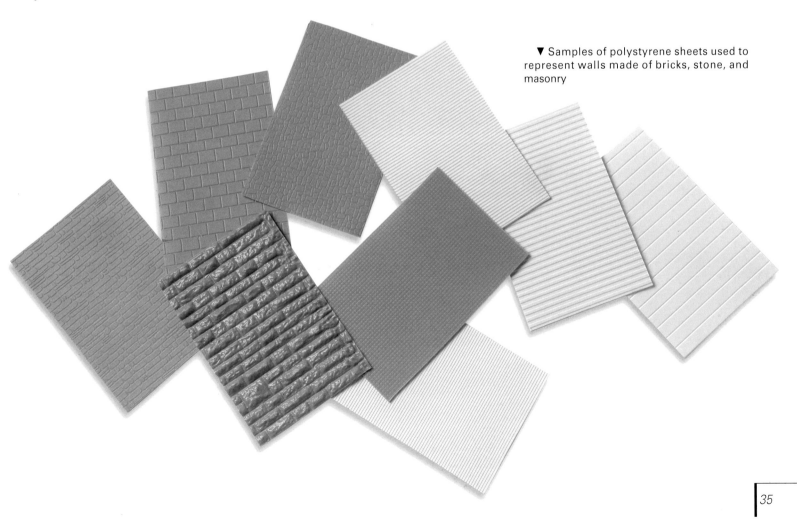

▼ Samples of polystyrene sheets used to represent walls made of bricks, stone, and masonry

# Other materials

## Sandpaper

Sandpaper is a sheet of paper, usually strong paper (although cloth or vulcanized fiber is also used), to which an abrasive material, called grit, has been fixed on the surface. It is available in a wide variety of weights and types. There are three main types, depending on the composition of the grit: silicon carbide; aluminum oxide (suitable for wood); and zirconium corundum. Sandpaper is numbered according to the number of particles of grit: the lower this number (amount per surface area), the larger the grit and the rougher the sanding. Therefore, if the number of particles is higher, the smaller they will be and the finer the sanding. The lowest numbers (for example, 40 or 0, depending on the type) correspond to coarse grit sandpaper and the highest numbers (400 or 6) to very fine grit sandpaper. When sanding by hand, the use of a sanding block is recommended. This is a block of wood, cork, or foam that holds the sandpaper in place, thus spreading the force more uniformly when sanding, which makes the work easier.

Sandpaper is used to polish the edges of the pieces that are to make up the model, as well as to smooth their surfaces. Acrylic should be sanded before starting work if it is to be finished with a coat of paint. Sandpaper is also used on pieces of clear, transparent acrylic to give them a matte surface and a translucent effect, and to polish wood that is used to make the base or stand of a model.

## Adhesives

### Two-part adhesives

Two-part adhesives are based on a thermostable polymer (polyepoxide or epoxy resin), which hardens due to a chemical reaction when it is mixed with a reagent (also called a hardener). These are extra-strong adhesives that enable rapid bonding, giving very hard-wearing bonds and resistance to chemical agents, heat, and humidity. They can be used to join different materials. Adhesion takes place rapidly, and the piece may be handled after just a few minutes, although in general it is best to wait at least 50 minutes; total drying, however, takes place in 12 hours, and the bonds reach their maximum strength within three days. This time varies depending on the manufacturer and environmental conditions.

### Methylene chloride

With the formula $CH_2Cl_2$, this substance is also called dichloromethane, methylene dichloride, or DCM. It is a colorless liquid, with a rather penetrating aroma. It is very volatile, soluble in alcohol and ether, and slightly soluble in water. It is mainly used as an industrial solvent and paint thinner, although in architectural modelmaking it is used for joining acrylic. It should be handled very carefully, and always kept in special receptacles for solvents fitted with a valve.

Methylene chloride should always be stored in correctly labelled, hermetically sealed containers in a ventilated place that is cool and dry, away from heat sources.

### Acrylic glues

Made specifically for joining acrylic, these adhesives have a viscous, gel-like consistency. They are transparent, with a slight yellowish tone, made with methylene chloride as a solvent. They are especially suitable for gluing without fissures and give fast joins; the pieces can be handled shortly after gluing and have excellent final resistance. Joins are stable 10 to 30 seconds after gluing and are totally dry after 3 hours, although these values vary depending on the manufacturer and environmental conditions. The contact surfaces must be cleaned with alcohol before the adhesive is applied. It should be used with care due to the presence of the solvent, and stored in labeled, tightly sealed containers in a cool, dry place.

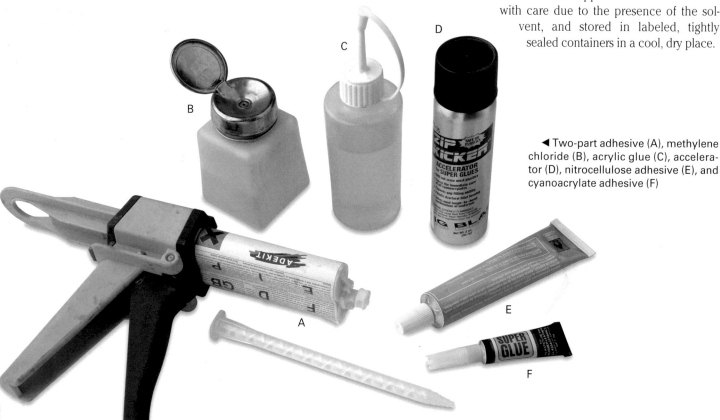

◀ Two-part adhesive (A), methylene chloride (B), acrylic glue (C), accelerator (D), nitrocellulose adhesive (E), and cyanoacrylate adhesive (F)

## Accelerators

Accelerators are catalysts that are specially formulated to speed up the adhesion of cyanoacrylate adhesives. They create extremely fast bonds in 6 or 8 seconds, depending on the manufacturer and environmental conditions. They do not alter the characteristics of the adhesives or their adhesive capacity. They can be applied to any type of surface, and are sold in liquid or aerosol form. The accelerator is applied to one of the surfaces to be joined and the adhesive to the other.

## Nitrocellulose adhesives

These are transparent adhesives with a very viscous, gel-like consistency. They dry as the solvent they contain evaporates, and as their gluing time is not too fast, some adjustments can be made. They are soluble in acetone. Bonds are strong, permanent, and resistant to humidity. These adhesives are used to join a wide variety of materials, and need to be left to dry for at least 24 hours.

## Cyanoacrylate Adhsives

These are very liquid glues with low viscosity. They work instantly, meaning that it is not possible to make last-minute adjustments; complete drying is effective within 24 hours. They are suitable for joining small pieces and for decorative details that require an instant bond. Bonds made with these adhesives are very strong.

## Silicone

Silicone is a semi-synthetic organosilicon polymer that is mainly used in architectural modelmaking to assemble display cases or covers, as well as bases and other elements.

## Polyurethane adhesives

These liquid adhesives are based on polyurethane (a polymer that is obtained by the condensation of polyols combined with polyisocyanates). They are caramel to clear beige in color. Bonds made with these adhesives have a fixing time of about 2 hours, and total drying is effective in 24 hours, depending on the type of adhesive, the manufacturer, and environmental conditions. The bonds made with this adhesive are impermeable and resistant to the elements, water, and chemical substances.

They are used to join all types of materials, and are especially suitable for gluing wood and filling in cracks. In architectural modelmaking, they are used to make bases or stands. They should be stored in well-closed containers, in a cool place out of direct sunlight.

## Contact adhesives

As their name suggests, these adhesives work through contact. They are made of synthetic rubber (generally neoprene) dissolved in a solvent; when this solvent evaporates, the adhesive sets. They should be handled in a well-ventilated place and kept away from sources of heat. They are very viscous, have great fixing power, and, once dry, are very strong. They provide an instant bond, meaning that it is not possible to make adjustments. Contact glue is applied to the two surfaces that you wish to join and allowed to dry for some minutes until it is no longer tacky to the touch. Depending on the type, manufacturer, and environmental conditions, these glues have an open time of 5 to 15 minutes, during which the layers of apparently dry adhesive can still be joined together. The total hardening time is about 72 hours.

## Polyvinyl acetate adhesives (PVA)

Polyvinyl acetate ($CH_3COO$ $CH:CH_2$)—commonly known as PVA, white glue, or carpenter's glue—is a clear, transparent resin. These adhesives are soluble in some organic solvents, are strongly adhesive, and form a very flexible film; they are resistant to the action of light and are stable against certain products. They are used for joining wood when making bases or stands. Total drying takes 24 hours.

## Aerosol adhesives

Aerosol adhesives are very suitable for the rapid fixing of light materials like paper or cardboard, as well as for gluing textiles onto a model. They are transparent and do not leave stains or residues on the surface. They offer good resistance to water and light. Reversible adhesives are available that allow material to be fixed temporarily, and removed it once the work is complete.

◀ Silicone (A), polyurethane adhesive (B), contact adhesive (C), PVA glue (D), aerosol adhesives (E)

▲ Double-sided adhesive tape (A), transparent adhesive tape (B), and drafting tape (C)

▶ Vinyl (A, B) and self-adhesive strips

## Adhesive tapes

Different types of adhesive tapes are used in architectural modelmaking. Everyday transparent adhesive tape is used to join pieces together temporarily so that they can be adjusted and the model assembled. Drafting tape is mainly used to protect certain areas by masking during the painting process, although it can also be used for temporary joins. Double-sided adhesive tape is used for final joins when fixing sheets of acrylic to the base, for joining pieces on the floor of the model, or for applying wooden veneers to the surface of the pieces, for example.

## Vinyl

Sheets of polyvinyl chloride (PVC) can be attached to the base material of an acrylic model with the help of an agent, in this case water with detergent. They are applied on a surface that has first been sprinkled with the agent. To ensure that they adhere correctly, excess water and any bubbles are removed by pressing firmly with a scraper from the center to the edges of the piece. Vinyl should be allowed to dry totally before further handling.

## Self-adhesive sheets

Self-adhesive plastic sheets are sold in different finishes (transparent or opaque, gloss or matte), colors, textures, and materials (cork or a velvety appearance). One of the sides contains a strong adhesive protected with paper; once this paper is removed, the plastic fixes permanently to any surface. They are used when making architectural models to give color or texture to a particular area or zone, adhering firmly to the base material.

## Paints

### Synthetics

Synthetic paints or enamels are generally made of alkydic resins and a solvent. They are opaque and give a silky surface once dry. Slow drying, they can be applied with a brush, roller, or spray gun. They are available in a wide variety of colors and finishes (matte, satin, gloss). They dry 3 to 4 hours after application and it is possible to repaint them after 16–24 hours have passed. They should be applied in thin layers, and then repainted to achieve the desired effect. If these enamels are to be applied with a spray gun, they should first be dissolved according to the instructions and proportions recommended by the manufacturer. Once the enamel has been applied, tools should be cleaned with a specific solvent or with universal solvent.

Some manufacturers have developed specific enamels for architectural modelmaking, and although their essential characteristics generally do not differ from other enamels, they are available in many finishes, such as metallic, hammered, or translucent. They can be used on a variety of materials, including acrylic and plastics, wood, metal, and cardboard. In general, they look dry to the touch 20–40 minutes after application (satin and matte) or after 1 or 2 hours (gloss); nevertheless, it is recommended that they be left to dry for at least 24 hours.

◀ Dyes (A), synthetic enamels (B), acrylic paints C)

▼ Spray paints for bodywork and cars in different finishes and colors

▼ Special paints for architectural model-making

## Acrylics

Acrylic paints are an emulsion of pigments in acrylic copolymers which have water as a solvent. They are therefore soluble in water, although once dry they are permanent and water-resistant. Faster drying than enamels, they can be applied with a brush, roller, or spray gun; in this case, they should first be diluted with 15 to 20 percent water. The final tone of the paint alters slightly when it dries, so initial trials are recommended. Once applied, the paint dries within 30 minutes to 1 hour, and it is possible to repaint within 5 or 6 hours. Tools should be cleaned with plenty of water immediately after use, and left to dry. Compared to enamels, these paints are safe for human health and the environment.

## Dyes

Dyes are colorants that are used to tint water-based paints (acrylics) and solvent-based synthetic enamels. They are highly concentrated and go a long way, meaning that only a small amount is necessary to give the desired tone to the paint. Once mixed, the result is a solid-colored paint, and the dye does not alter the finish. It is recommended that no more than a proportion of 5 percent of dye is added to the paint; adding too much may affect its properties.

## Paint for bodywork for cars

Paints specifically designed for bodywork and cars are also used in architectural model-making. These are special paints based on acrylic enamels in an aerosol, sold in a wide range of colors and finishes. They offer solid and, in general, very saturated colors, are easy to apply, adhere well, and dry quickly. They come in a wide variety of opaque and transparent colors, with multiple finishes, as well as metallic (gold, silver, chrome, bronze), pearlized metallic, anodized, and even fluorescent colors, among others.

# Trees, vegetation, and ground surfaces

The creation of architectural models often requires representing natural elements such as vegetation and ground surfaces. In the first case, an endless array of materials can be used—including foam and natural or artificial sponges—to create our own trees and hedges according to the needs of each project, although the fastest and most practical option is to use prefabricated pieces. Different types of trees are sold that represent a wide variety of species, made in brass or foam, with dimensions of between ³⁄₁₆ to 5 or 6 in (6 to 125 or 160 mm) in height. In each case, the most appropriate size for the scale of the model should be chosen, taking into account that real trees are almost never at the same scale as the building and can be larger or smaller. Tree crowns can also be purchased in different shades of foam with diameters that vary from ½ to 1½ in (13 to 38 mm).

These can be used to make trees and hedges in the workshop, according to the specific needs of each project. Hedges can be made in polyurethane sheets of different densities dyed in various shades of green, cut to the right size, as can dyed natural moss or dyed grass tufts. Finally, gravel is used to represent some ground surfaces. It is sold in fine, medium, or coarse grains.

◄ Foam sheets and tree tops

◄ Foam (A, B), moss (C), grass tufts (D), and ground grass (E)

▲ Selection of gravel

▼ Different types of trees

## SOME EXAMPLES OF PREFABRICATED ITEMS

### STAIRCASES

Staircases (A, B), steps (C), and spiral staircase (D), unassembled, made in polystyrene. Industrial staircases (E) made in ABS.

| TYPES | SCALES |
|---|---|
| Staircases at 34° | 1:50, 1:100, 1:200, 1:500 |
| Staircases at 17° | 1:50, 1:100, 1:200, 1:500 |
| Spiral staircases | 1:25, 1:50, 1:100, 1:200 |
| Steps | 1:25, 1:50, 1:100, 1:200 |
| Industrial staircases | 1:16, 1:25, 1:33, 1:50, 1:100, 1:200 |

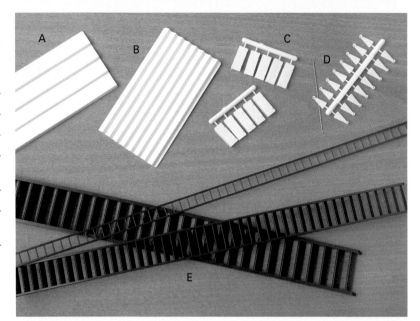

### RAILINGS, FENCES, AND BALUSTRADES

Railings in brass (A), balustrade in polystyrene (B), fences in polystyrene (C), and industrial railings in ABS (D).

| TYPES | SCALES |
|---|---|
| Railings | 1:100, 1:200, 1:500 |
| Industrial railings | 1:15, 1:25, 1:33, 1:50, 1:100, 1:200 |

Other elements are sold according to dimensions.

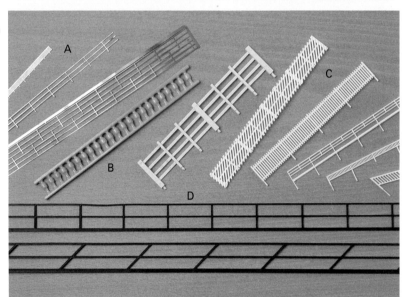

### STREET FURNITURE

Double lamppost (A) and single-arm street lamp (B, C) and double-arm street lamp (D) in polystyrene.

| TYPES | SCALES |
|---|---|
| Double lampposts | 1:50, 1:100 |
| Street lamps | 1:100, 1:200, 1:500 |

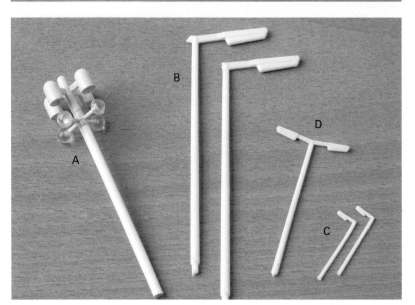

## SOME EXAMPLES OF PREFABRICATED ITEMS

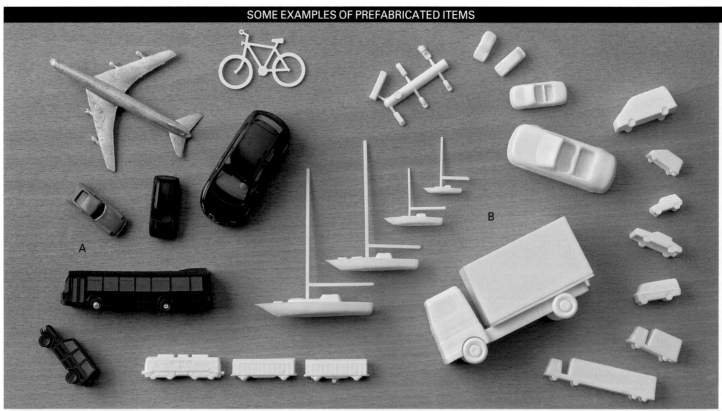

## MEANS OF TRANSPORT

Airplanes, buses, and cars in painted metal (A), bicycle, trains, boats, trucks, and cars in polystyrene (B).

| TYPES | SCALES |
| --- | --- |
| Airplanes | 1:1.000 |
| Trains | 1:500 |
| Boats | Sold according to dimensions. |
| Cars | 1:50, 1:87, 1:100, 1:150, 1:200, 1:250, 1:333, 1:400, 1:500, 1:1.000 |
| Buses | 1:200, 1:400, 1:500 |
| Trucks | 1:100, 1:200, 1:400, 1:500 |
| Bicycles | 1:50, 1:100, 1:150, 1:200 |

## FURNITURE

Loungers, chairs, and armchairs in polystyrene (A), theater seats in PVC (B). Home and office furniture (C) and sanitary ware in polystyrene (D).

| TYPES | SCALES |
| --- | --- |
| Garden furniture | 1:25, 1:33, 1:50, 1:100, 1:200 |
| Tables | 1:20, 1:25, 1:33, 1:50, 1:100 |
| Armchairs | 1:25, 1:100 |
| Chairs | 1:20, 1:25, 1:50, 1:100 |
| Theater seats | 1:25, 1:50, 1:100 |
| Office, dining-room, bedroom, and kitchen furniture | 1:25, 1:50 |
| Sanitary ware | 1:25, 1:33, 1:50, 1:100 |

## HUMAN FIGURES

Figures and silhouettes in polystyrene.

| TYPES | SCALES |
|---|---|
| Figures | 1:25, 1:50, 1:100, 1:200 |
| Silhouettes | 1:50, 1:75, 1:100, 1:150, 1:200, 1:250, 1:333, 1:400, 1:500 |

# Lighting materials

Architectural models sometimes add lighting to the representation, which involves specific materials. Different types of lamps can be used, including dichroic lamps, fluorescent tubes, and LEDs (light-emitting diodes). Electroluminescent panels are also useful. These are very thin panels covered with a layer of optical coating, the most common being manganese-doped zinc sulfide (ZnS:Mn), which emits light in response to an electrical current crossing it or as a result of a strong electrical field. Its greatest inconvenience is its high cost, as well as the fact that it is difficult to source. Its main advantage is that interesting effects can be achieved. Installing lighting requires that appropriate systems be fitted and used, such as transformers, ballast, and starters in the case of fluorescent tubes, sockets, and switches.

▼ Transformers (A, B), ballast for fluorescent tubes (C), compact fluorescent lamp (D), dichroic lamp (E), LEDs (F), and electroluminescent panels (G)

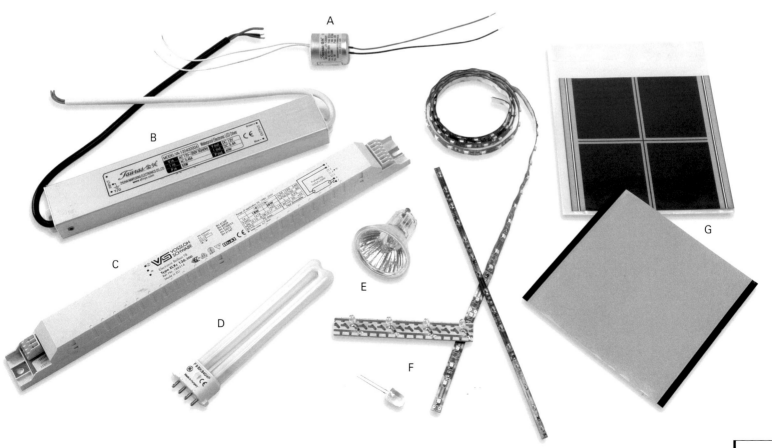

# Architectural models in a variety of materials

One of the most interesting possibilities when making architectural models is the potential of different, innovative materials. These can make up the whole model or be combined with traditional materials like wood. Either way, the material plays a key role in the representation, with considerable expressive value. Although it is possible to make any type of model with a mix of materials, in general these are conceptual and even abstract representations, making them a first-class resource when creating project models for competitions, for example. The freedom to choose and use materials independently of the literal physical representation favors effects and contrasts in which the relationships between the parts is emphasized. Some examples of architectural models made with a range of different materials are shown here, as well as others made with innovative materials that are radically different from those traditionally used in presentation models.

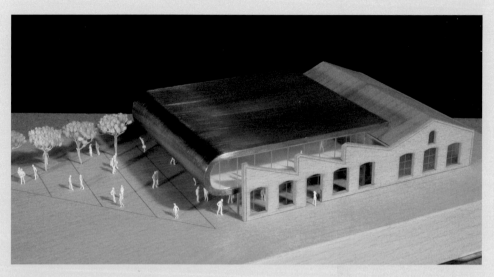

▲ Architectural model of a design to adapt a building in Colònia Güell, Santa Coloma de Cervelló, Barcelona, Alonso, Balaguer y Arquitectos Asociados. Architectural model of beech and copper made by Maquet-barna (scale 1:200), 2007. A traditional material, wood, was used to create the presentation model, along with a more innovative material, copper.

▼ Architectural model of the project for the headquarters of the Government of Andorra, Ramon Sanabria, architect. Architectural model of acrylic and natural stones, made by Maquet-barna (scale 1: 200), 2003. Natural materials were used in this presentation model (the stones were applied and then polished) to suggest the face of the walls of the original building (at top), as well as those of the walls on the new work.

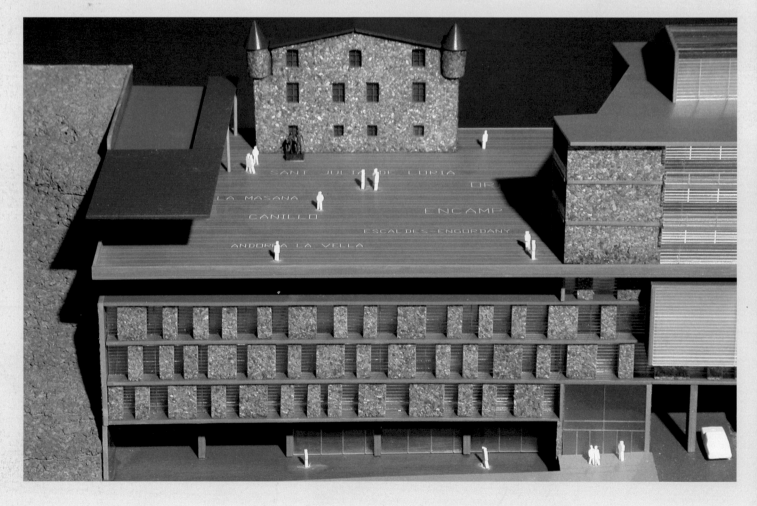

◀ Architectural model of a car park in Mallorca, Antonio García Ruiz, architect. Architectural model of zinc, metal, and acrylic made by Maquet-barna (scale 1: 400), 2005. The final result has great expressive power.

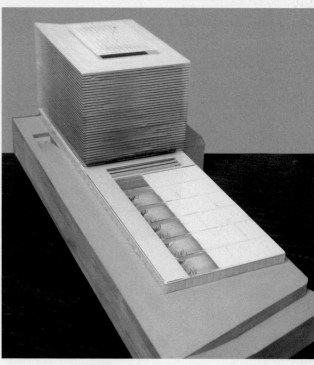

▶ Detail of the car park where the base and elements made of zinc are visible, while the fences and vegetation were created with metallic mesh and metal, respectively. The pergolas and other elements were made of acrylic.

▲▶ Architectural model of a building at Bocconi University, Milan, Carlos Ferrater, architect. Architectural model of acrylic made by Maquet-barna (scale 1:200), 2003. Two views of the model, made of acrylic to suggest glass.

◄ Architectural model of the library buildings and book depository at the headquarters of the regional government of Bizkaia in Bilbao, IMB Arquitectos. Architectural model of beech and acrylic made by Maquet-barna (scale 1:200), 2003. In representation models, the work that is to be done can be highlighted by using dramatically different materials. Here, wood was used to broadly represent existing buildings, while the new architectural work was made of acrylic.

▼ Detail of the book depository, represented with strongly realistic components.

► Architectural model of the Castilla y León Court Building, León, Ramón Fernández Alonso Borrajo, architect. Architectural model of wood made by Maquet-barna (scale 1:200), 2005. On this occasion, an initial version of the model was made with a traditional material.

► Architectural model of the Castilla y León Court Building, Ramón Fernández Alonso Borrajo, architect. Architectural model of stainless steel and acrylic made by Maquet-barna (scale 1:200), 2005. The difference between the expressive values of this steel and acrylic architectural model can be seen in relation to the model above.

# Hand tools

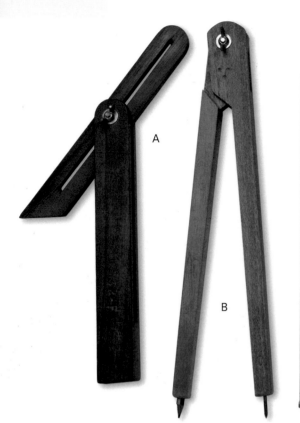

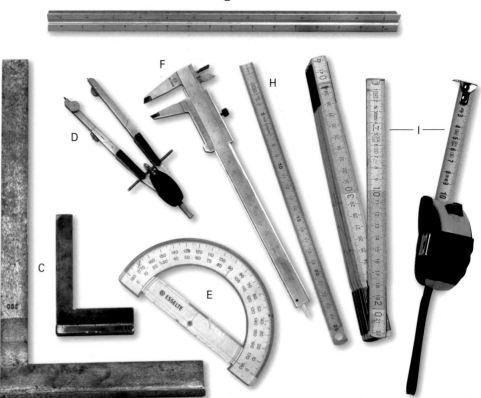

▲ Bevel gauge (A), compass (B and D), set squares (C), protractor (E), calipers (F), scale ruler (G), ruler (H), and tape measures (I)

## Tools to measure, convert, mark, draw, and check

### Tape measure and ruler

These are used to take measurements. The ruler is also used to draw straight lines and check flat surfaces.

### Scale ruler

Also called an architect's scale, this is a special ruler on which the different scales used to measure and convert scales are represented. Different models are available, but the most usual consists of a triangular ruler that shows different calibrated scales. The correct scale can be seen by simply turning the scale ruler.

### Calipers

Calipers consist of a fixed ruler and a movable scale that slides along its length. They are used for very small and precise measurements.

### Compass and protractor

The compass is used to draw and mark curves and circumferences, as well as to measure and transfer measurements and check the diameters of pieces. The protractor is a drawing instrument that is usually made of transparent plastic. It is semicircular in shape and etched with graduations to 180°, although there are also circular protractors with graduations to 360°. Protractors are used to measure and create angles.

### Set square and bevel gauge

A set square is a metal instrument with two arms at a right angle. It is used to accurately check the right angles and edges of pieces. A bevel gauge is made up of two rulers joined by a fixed nut on one of the rulers, around which the other slides. It is used to draw, transfer, and check angles.

## Tools to cut, separate, and file

### Scalpel and utility knife

A scalpel is a surgical instrument that can be used to make precise, clean, deep cuts. It is made up of a steel knife mounted on a handle of the same material. A utility knife or disposable blade knife consists of a handle, usually of plastic, with a cutting blade inserted into it. This can be removed and dis-

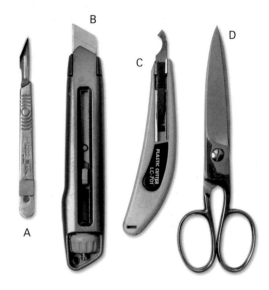

▲ Scalpel (A), utility knife (B), utility knife for plastics (C), and scissors (D)

posed of as necessary. These knives are used to make precise cuts. Some utility knives are specifically designed to cut plastics, and are fitted with a special blade.

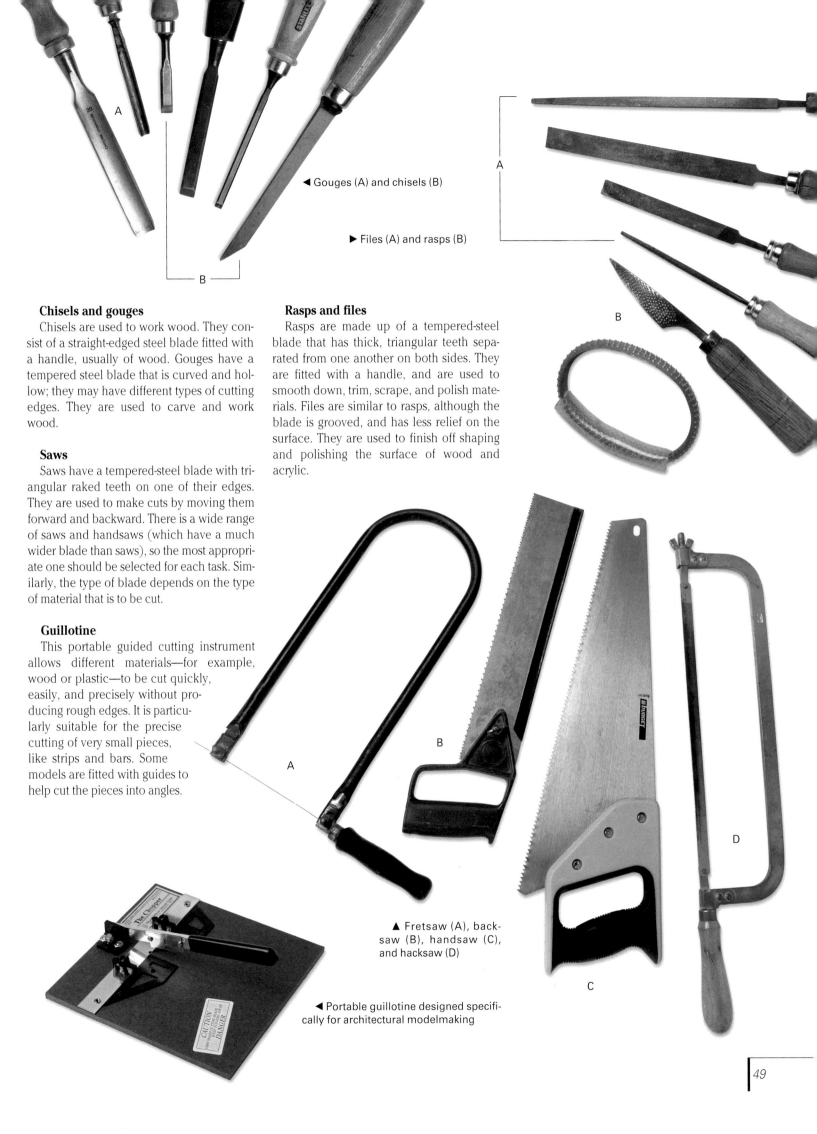

◀ Gouges (A) and chisels (B)

▶ Files (A) and rasps (B)

## Chisels and gouges

Chisels are used to work wood. They consist of a straight-edged steel blade fitted with a handle, usually of wood. Gouges have a tempered steel blade that is curved and hollow; they may have different types of cutting edges. They are used to carve and work wood.

## Saws

Saws have a tempered-steel blade with triangular raked teeth on one of their edges. They are used to make cuts by moving them forward and backward. There is a wide range of saws and handsaws (which have a much wider blade than saws), so the most appropriate one should be selected for each task. Similarly, the type of blade depends on the type of material that is to be cut.

## Guillotine

This portable guided cutting instrument allows different materials—for example, wood or plastic—to be cut quickly, easily, and precisely without producing rough edges. It is particularly suitable for the precise cutting of very small pieces, like strips and bars. Some models are fitted with guides to help cut the pieces into angles.

## Rasps and files

Rasps are made up of a tempered-steel blade that has thick, triangular teeth separated from one another on both sides. They are fitted with a handle, and are used to smooth down, trim, scrape, and polish materials. Files are similar to rasps, although the blade is grooved, and has less relief on the surface. They are used to finish off shaping and polishing the surface of wood and acrylic.

▲ Fretsaw (A), backsaw (B), handsaw (C), and hacksaw (D)

◀ Portable guillotine designed specifically for architectural modelmaking

▼ Clothes pins (A), clamps for architectural modelmaking (B), retaining rings (C and D), and clamps (E, F and G).

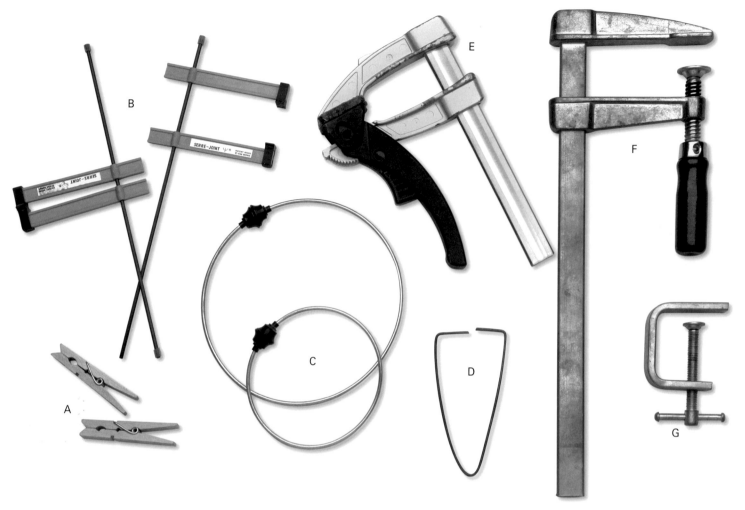

# Tools to hold and apply pressure

### Clamps and retaining rings

Clamps are used to hold, secure, and apply pressure to model pieces. They are usually made of iron, and consist of two jaws. One of these jaws is movable and adjustable and the other is fixed; both are joined by a guide. Special clamps made of plastic are available for working with small model parts. Retaining rings are made up of a thick steel wire that closes back on itself thanks to the elasticity of the material. Wooden clothes pins may also be used to hold items in place.

### Roller scrapers

Rollers are used to roll and fix vinyl onto the surface of a material. Scrapers are used to apply products or to roll out and smooth vinyl and self-adhesive sheets. They have either a plastic or steel blade, depending on the model. Wads of felt can also be used for this purpose.

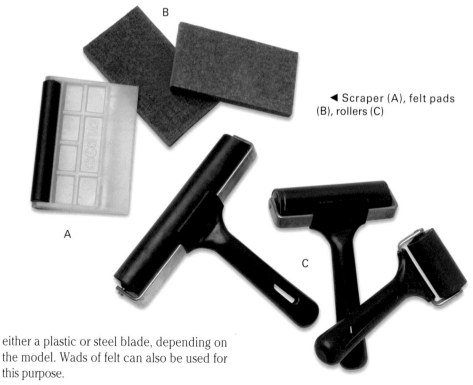

◀ Scraper (A), felt pads (B), rollers (C)

### Tweezers and push pins

Tweezers are useful during architectural modelmaking to handle small pieces and, in general, in all processes that require precision. Push pins are used to fix small items temporarily and provisionally.

## Additional tools

### Screwdrivers and wrenches

Screwdrivers are made of an iron bar with a tip that matches the shape of the screw head it is designed to be used with; they have a wooden or plastic handle and their purpose is to insert and remove screws. When making certain parts of the model, such as the base, other tools may be needed to tighten or loosen screws, for example, monkey wrenches or hex keys (often known as Allen keys).

### Pliers and shears

Pliers are like pincers with square or round tips; they are used to cut and fold materials. Shears are similar to a pair of scissors; they are fitted with blades that safely and efficiently cut thin sheets of plastic and metal.

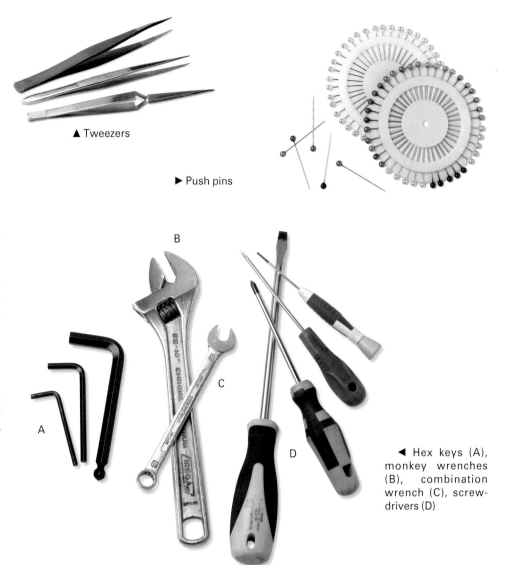

▲ Tweezers

► Push pins

◄ Hex keys (A), monkey wrenches (B), combination wrench (C), screwdrivers (D)

► Shears (A) and pliers (B)

# Machines

◀ Jigsaw

## Machines for cutting

To cut wood or plastic, it is necessary to use a saw. A table saw has a robust base and a table above; a mechanism located inside the frame causes the cutting blade or saw that projects out of the table center to move. The cut is made as the board moves forward. The height and position of the cutting blade can be adjusted, depending on the model and the manufacturer; in addition, some saws have special systems to remove shavings and dust. A table extension is very useful when working with large boards.

A band saw is made up of a base with a table and a vertical arm fitted with a long, narrow, and flexible cutting blade in an upright position that moves in a continuous sliding motion. A jigsaw is an electric tool that enables fast sawing and can be used to make large cuts. It

▼ Table saw, with table extension for large boards and extraction system

works through the up-and-down movement of a toothed blade that produces the cut. The blades are interchangeable, which allows the user to determine the most suitable blade in terms of size and teeth, depending on the cut that is to be made.

## Machines for smoothing and polishing

A tabletop polishing machine is used to polish and smooth small pieces and, in general, to finish fine details. It consists of a base and table with a vertical abrasive disc that rotates at high speed. Electric sanders enable large surfaces to be sanded without effort. They could be orbital sanders, in which a disc rotates, or belt sanders, fitted with a continuous abrasive belt. One evolution of belt sanders is the so-called mini-belt sander; in essence, this is similar to the larger version, but it is fitted with a narrow abrasive belt and an accessory that allows the user to reach difficult areas. An electric planer is used to smooth wood; it has a flat-bottomed surface and is fitted with a rotating drum with cutting blades.

▼ Band saw

▶ Tabletop polishing machine

▲ Plane

◀ Sander

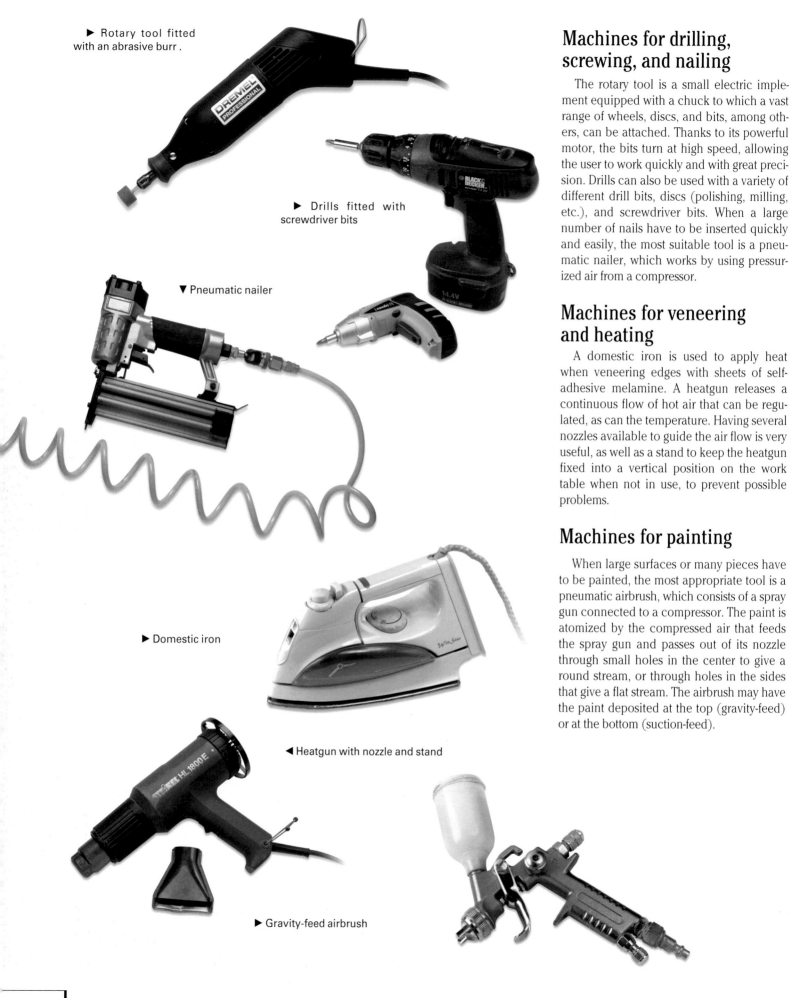

► Rotary tool fitted with an abrasive burr .

► Drills fitted with screwdriver bits

▼ Pneumatic nailer

► Domestic iron

◄ Heatgun with nozzle and stand

► Gravity-feed airbrush

# Machines for drilling, screwing, and nailing

The rotary tool is a small electric implement equipped with a chuck to which a vast range of wheels, discs, and bits, among others, can be attached. Thanks to its powerful motor, the bits turn at high speed, allowing the user to work quickly and with great precision. Drills can also be used with a variety of different drill bits, discs (polishing, milling, etc.), and screwdriver bits. When a large number of nails have to be inserted quickly and easily, the most suitable tool is a pneumatic nailer, which works by using pressurized air from a compressor.

# Machines for veneering and heating

A domestic iron is used to apply heat when veneering edges with sheets of self-adhesive melamine. A heatgun releases a continuous flow of hot air that can be regulated, as can the temperature. Having several nozzles available to guide the air flow is very useful, as well as a stand to keep the heatgun fixed into a vertical position on the work table when not in use, to prevent possible problems.

# Machines for painting

When large surfaces or many pieces have to be painted, the most appropriate tool is a pneumatic airbrush, which consists of a spray gun connected to a compressor. The paint is atomized by the compressed air that feeds the spray gun and passes out of its nozzle through small holes in the center to give a round stream, or through holes in the sides that give a flat stream. The airbrush may have the paint deposited at the top (gravity-feed) or at the bottom (suction-feed).

# Laser cutter

The laser cutter is a high-precision machine that is used to cut, engrave, and trim plastics, wood, and other materials. It consists of a workstation with an articulated arm fitted with a laser beam and a cutting table with a mesh or honeycomb base. The material that is to be worked is placed on this surface. The operation of the laser is regulated and controlled by a computer program. The chosen design is programmed into the computer, and the values and parameters—such as speed, power, resolution, and density—are set. In fact, it works in a similar manner to any printer.

To start the work, the material is first correctly positioned on the table following the design that has been fed into the computer program; the design is then printed from the program, and once in operation, the beam moves across the material following the design. The light from the laser is turned into heat energy that engraves or cuts the material, depending on the power that has been programmed in.

Laser-cutting machines require a fume extraction system to expel the fumes that are generated. In the workshop, they should be placed in a separate room or a special space away from the other work areas, and the necessary safety precautious should be taken while they are in use. Although this equipment is very costly due to the technology and safety requirements involved, small-sized portable laser-cutting machines are available in a variety of basic compact models that are more affordable for professional teams who need to cut out large pieces.

▼ Laser cutter and engraver, showing the fume extraction system and the computer that controls the machine

*T*his section summarizes the key technical aspects involved in creating architectural models. The discipline requires knowledge and understanding of certain concepts without which any attempt to do the work would be fruitless. It is therefore essential that we understand the theory behind producing models before starting work. The section that follows consists of two parts. In the first part, these concepts are explained in detail, giving practical examples to support and clarify the theory; several summary tables are included as a reference, including one on the different phases involved in a project that should be helpful for all kinds of models. In the second part, key techniques are shown from a practical viewpoint. The processes explained here complement those given in the step-by-step guides that follow in the final section.

# Technical
## aspects

# Initial considerations

## Scale

Scale is the size or proportion of a plan or architectural model or, in other words, the proportions between the dimensions of its parts and the parts of the building or architectural project and the surroundings that it represents. It therefore describes the reduction ratio between reality and the architectural model that represents it. The scale chosen will depend on various factors: the type of model and how it is represented; how the project is defined; the use to which the model will be put; and the materials that are to make it up. Clearly, the same scale would not be used to represent a building or a part of it (a façade, for example) as to represent work to be done on a site that would include a topographic representation of a large area. The most common scales according to model type are shown in the table below.

The reduction ratio is calculated by dividing all the measurements of the design that we wish to represent by a factor greater than 1, as the scale 1:1 represents actual size. It is therefore possible to work out a scale, change it, or calculate the actual measurement of a dimension by doing some simple mathematical calculations. In the case of a 1:500 scale, the expression of the scale corresponds to a fraction in which the numerator or dividend corresponds to one unit of the plan, and the denominator corresponds to 500 units in real terms. More simply put, one unit in model scale equals a given length in real terms.

### Measurement conversion

Once the theoretical concepts have been absorbed, it should not be difficult to move from one scale to another, find out the real measurements of any element on the basis of its scale, or transfer the real dimensions to a certain scale. A scale ruler can be used to avoid the need for constant mathematical calculations, although with daily practice it is possible to acquire sufficient mental agility to rapidly calculate dimensions. Some examples of converting measurements using a scale ruler are given to help the reader, although this can be done through the use of the right computations.

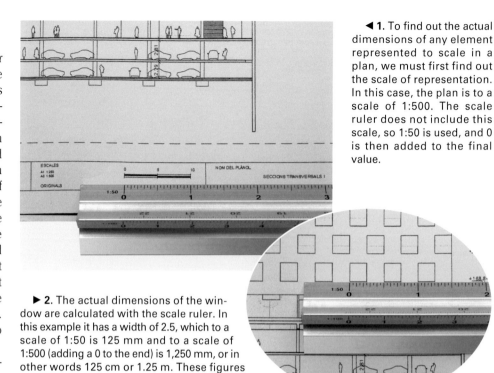

◄ **1.** To find out the actual dimensions of any element represented to scale in a plan, we must first find out the scale of representation. In this case, the plan is to a scale of 1:500. The scale ruler does not include this scale, so 1:50 is used, and 0 is then added to the final value.

▶ **2.** The actual dimensions of the window are calculated with the scale ruler. In this example it has a width of 2.5, which to a scale of 1:50 is 125 mm and to a scale of 1:500 (adding a 0 to the end) is 1,250 mm, or in other words 125 cm or 1.25 m. These figures correspond to the dimensions of the apertures and windows in an office building.

| SCALES ACCORDING TO THE TYPE OF ARCHITECTURAL MODEL | | |
|---|---|---|
| **Type of model** | | **Scale** |
| Topographic | Site | $\frac{1}{32}$" = 1' or $\frac{1}{64}$" = 1" in the United States 1:5,000, 1:2,000, and 1:1,000 |
| | Landscaping and natural landscapes | 1:2,500, 1:1,000, and 1:500 The scale 1:5,000 is also used in certain cases |
| | Garden | 1:500, 1:200, and 1:100 It is also possible to use the scale 1:50 |
| Buildings | Urban planning | 1:1,000 and 1:500 It is also possible to use the scale 1:200 |
| | Layout plans | 1:1,000 to 1:2,500 |
| | Partial or detail planning model | 1:500 to 1:200 |
| | Urban design | 1:200 to 1:50 |
| | Building with layout | $\frac{1}{16}$" = 1', $\frac{1}{8}$" = 1' in the United States 1:500, 1:200, and 1:100 |
| | Building without layout | 1:100 to 1:50 |
| | Interiors | 1:100 to 1:20 |
| | Details | $\frac{1}{2}$" = 1', 1" = 1' in the United States 1:20 to 1:5 1:1 models can also be made |

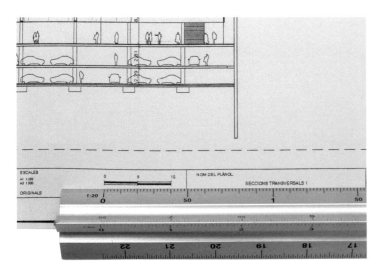

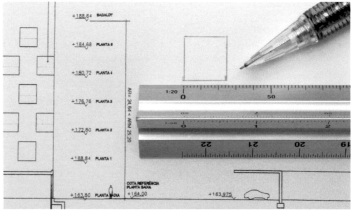

◄ **3.** It is also a simple task to transfer the dimensions of any element to another scale. Following the previous example, in order to make it easier to understand, the window shown is converted from a scale of 1:500 to 1:200. The scale ruler does not have a scale of 1:200, so 1:20 is used and a 0 added to the final value.

▲ **4.** The scale of 1:200 is greater than 1:500, here 1 mm on the plan corresponds to 200 mm of reality. The window is drawn following the dimensions of the representation at a scale of 1:500. We can see that the width of the 2.5 window at a scale of 1:200 is much greater than at the original scale.

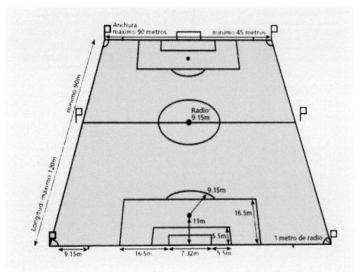

◄ **5.** Another example is found in the representation of real elements to a certain scale. Here, a football field of 100 m long and 70 m wide was to be represented at a scale of 1:1,000.

▼ **6.** The scale ruler is used with the scale of 1:100, and a 0 is also added to the final value. The outline of the field is drawn: at a scale of 1:100, 100 m (10,000 cm) correspond to 10 cm on the plan and the width of 70 m corresponds to 7 cm on the plan.

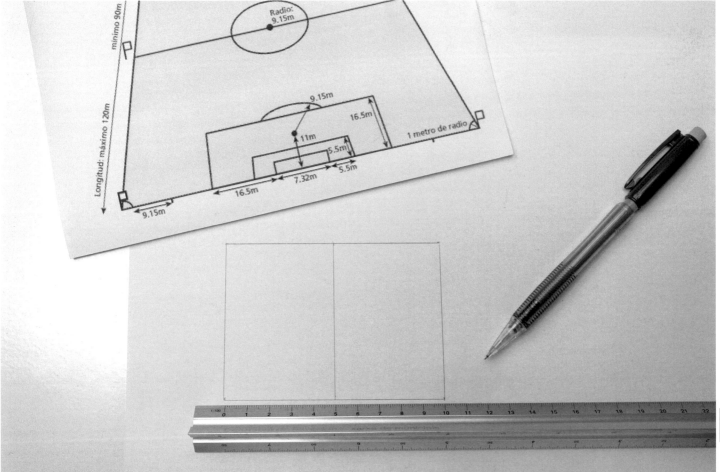

# The phases of a project

| PHASES IN THE CREATION AND PRODUCTION OF AN ARCHITECTURAL MODEL | | | |
|---|---|---|---|
| Order | Design enters the workshop | | |
| Study of the design | Study of the design documentation: plans on paper or in computer format, as well as computer graphic representations (renders) or perspectives | Establishing the process and work time | |
| | | Establishing the scale (if this is not defined in the design) and dimensions of the model | |
| | | Establishing the needs of: | Human resources |
| | | | Materials and tools |
| | | | Any special pieces or materials |
| | | | Others |
| Preparatory work | Display case | Ordering the display case from a specialist company | Receipt of the display case |
| | | Creation of the display case in the workshop | |
| | Base or stand | Production of the base or stand by an external company | Receipt of the stand |
| | | Creation of the stand in the workshop | |
| Preparatory cutting work | Preparation of the plans needed for cutting | | |
| | Handling and preparation of computer files needed for laser cutting | | |
| Production of pieces | Cutting | | |
| | Milling | | |
| | Engraving | | |
| | Cutting prefabricated pieces | | |
| | Others | | |
| Painting | In some projects, some pieces may need to be painted before assembly | | |
| Initial assembly | Construction of the frame, if required | | |
| | Production and construction of the topography | | |
| | Construction of the surroundings | | |
| | Others | | |
| | Painting the topography or the surroundings | | |
| Assembly | Initial tests made to check the pieces before starting assembly | | |
| | Assembly of the building | | |
| | In some projects, the partially or totally assembled elements that make up the building may need painting | | |
| | Assembly of auxiliary elements and the surroundings, if necessary | | |
| Finishes and positioning | Making the finishes of the surroundings: green areas, gravel or another type | | |
| | Veneering or painting the stand or base, if required | | |
| | Painting the surface or retouching existing paintwork | | |
| | Positioning and attaching the building and other elements in the surroundings | | |
| | Positioning ornamental elements and legends | | |

| General finishes | Assembly of the display case supports |
| | Assembly of the legs |
| | Application of the modelmaker's logo or name |
| | Positioning and fixing the display case |
| | Production of the packing case, if necessary |
| Delivery of model | Delivery of the model and unpacking, if necessary |
| Document archive | Design (plans, computer files, renders, etc.), financial and photographic documentation of the process (if this exists) |

These phases are merely an indication of how to create and produce an architectural model. Every design will involve different specific processes depending on its nature and characteristics. These processes vary for each model.

# Preparing plans

The preparation of plans is a key aspect prior to starting work on any architectural model. Indeed, it is an essential process upon which the success of the work will directly depend. Sufficient information should be available to produce the model using topographic plans of the environment (if they exist) and floor plans of the building, as well as the elevations corresponding to all of the sides and sections. Access to detailed plans for some elements may also be necessary. It is useful to have the plans at the right scale, that is, the same scale as the model. Otherwise, plans can be altered by using reprographic techniques (photocopies) or a computer program, if they reach the workshop in a digital format. In addition, the number of copies available must be checked if it is necessary to use any of the plans as a kind of template.

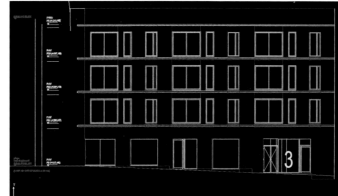

◄ 1. Creating plans in a digital format simplifies the preparation of the work. A partial view of the elevation of one of the façades of a building can be seen here. The building's apertures and the woodwork of windows and doors are also shown.

► 2. Computer-aided design allows designers to manage the information contained in the plan. This helps create the files needed to subsequently cut the pieces by laser. In this case, the work is done in layers, starting with the enclosures (shown by green lines).

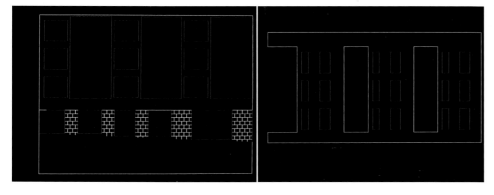

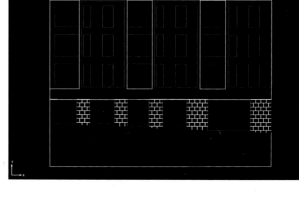

◄ 3. Next, the different levels of the façade's apertures are also separated into layers; this gives us the shapes of the pieces, ready to cut using the laser.

# Preparing materials

Once the preparation of the plans and documents that accompany the project is completed, the materials that will be used to make the model are prepared. Acrylic and wood are dealt with in a similar way. Both materials are cut with a saw (manual or electric) and can be engraved by laser. It is possible to use a laser to cut acrylic that has been previously veneered with wood, and also to engrave the top veneer. Compared to veneers and some types of wood, acrylic is usually covered with a coat of paint to represent the building's color and texture. To guarantee that the paint layer adheres to the acrylic, the acrylic should first be sanded thoroughly; otherwise the paint does not set and runs off the surface of the material.

▲ 1. The pieces of wood and acrylic are cut with a saw, in this case a circular saw. The acrylic is cut while it still has its backing sheets in place; these are later removed after the last cut is made and before laser engraving or assembly of the piece, depending on the processes involved in making the model.

▲ 2. If the acrylic is to be painted, the surface will first need sanding thoroughly with an electric sander or by manually sanding.

◄ 3. Color tests on the base material (in this case white opaque acrylic, sanded beforehand) are recommended to check that the tone of the paint matches the actual materials, here the color of the brick at the back and the stone at the front.

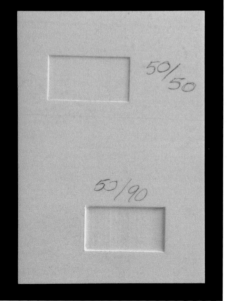

◄ Acrylic can be engraved using a laser cutter, adjusting the power of the laser and the speed. Vector engraving uses vectors to follow the lines of the pattern to be engraved, and raster engraving uses dots to simulate lines through the use of line-by-line movements. Before engraving any piece, it is worth carrying out tests to establish the engraving depth. Here, two tests were carried out, the first with the laser at a speed of 50 and a power of 50, and the second with the same speed and a power of 90; the engraving depth was greater.

▶ Wood and veneers can also be engraved by laser. Here, several tests were made on a piece of sapele veneer, with the laser programmed at a speed of 50 and a power of 25, 17, 12, and 8 respectively, to achieve the required effect.

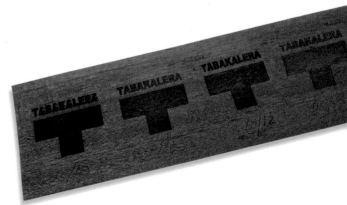

Before starting the final assembly of the model, it is essential to make trial runs, for example, by temporarily fixing together the parts of the building. This process is vital for ensuring that the work is appropriate for the project, as well as for checking that the pieces fit correctly and to detect possible faults or problems; this helps us correct any defects before starting work. Although this process may seem unnecessary, it should never be omitted, because it affects the efficiency and quality of the work.

▶ **1.** This example shows the system followed in the initial presentation of an architectural model for a building, made by superimposing floors and other elements. The first step consists of attaching the lower floor to the base and one of the façade elements with adhesive tape.

▼ **2.** The first floor is assembled, and attached with adhesive tape.

◀ **3.** The building's central staircase, which has previously been assembled using adhesive tape, is fixed into place.

▲ **4.** The pieces that make up the building are checked to ensure that they fit; they are joined firmly with adhesive tape, and the angles are checked with the square.

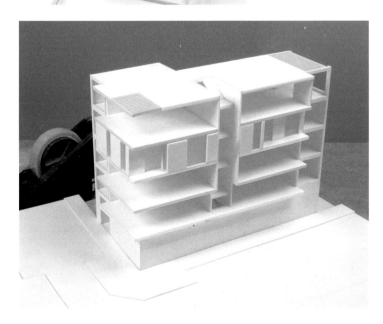

◀ **5.** Here, the initial presentation requires that the entire building structure be assembled.

# Adhesives

| DIFFERENT TYPES ACCORDING TO THEIR USE AND COMPONENTS | | |
|---|---|---|
| **Adhesives** | **Use** | **Specifications** |
| Two-part adhesives | Suitable for joining different materials, they give very strong and resistant bonds | Indicated for gluing a wide variety of materials, such as plastic, wood, metal, and glass. They are also used to attach optical fiber in models, as these adhesives do not degrade its plastic material. |
| Methylene chloride | Suitable for joining acrylic and poly-styrene. Indicated for fine joins, as it penetrates the cracks and gaps between the pieces by capillary action | Strictly speaking, this is a solvent that is used like an adhesive. It acts by superficially dissolving plastics, which bind closely. Care should be taken with clear or shiny plastics, as it muddies them and affects the shine, respectively. Methylene chloride is not indicated for joining PVC sheets. It is not recommended for joining acrylic sheets, surface to surface, as it only partially penetrates the sides, and the joins are not reliable. |
| Acrylic glues | Suitable for joining pieces of acrylic and attaching this material to other porous surfaces, including wood or foam board | They are quite thick and viscous, making them suitable to glue joins that need filling, such as open bevelled edges. They are also suitable for pieces that require strong joins and to join acrylic to another surface, e.g., the underside of a building to the base of the model. It is worth remembering that the solvent in the glue dissolves plastic superficially. The drying time is somewhat longer than that of methylene chloride, meaning that adjustments can be made. Acrylic glues dissolve polystyrene. They are not recommended for joining acrylic sheets surface to surface, as the adhesive does not dry (through evaporation of the solvent) in the center of the sheets. The solvent attacks the plastic, and may dissolve the center of the sheets. |
| Nitrocellulose adhesives | Suitable for joining small elements | Indicated for joining small painted elements, as they dissolve the paint less than other adhesives (see the general observations at the foot of the table). Somewhat slower to dry than the other adhesives, which allows adjustments to be made. |

| Adhesives | Use | Specifications |
|---|---|---|
| Cyanoacrylate adhesives | Suitable for instant joins of small pieces and details | Once dry, although the joins are resistant, they are not elastic, meaning that they do not tolerate possible impacts.<br><br>It is not possible to join pieces painted with a marker pen or aerosol.<br><br>Applying a small amount of adhesive to the join area is sufficient; too much would release vapors and leave a white layer on the pieces, which can be removed with acetone . |
| Polyurethane adhesives | Suitable for joining a wide range of materials to one another (wood + wood, wood + plastic, plastic + plastic, metal + plastic, etc.) | Slow drying; there is a longer time frame for adjustments compared to other adhesives.<br><br>They are used to join surfaces of some parts of the model, such as bodies of water or watercourses, which have been painted where the join needs to be made. |
| Contact adhesives | Suitable for joining surfaces of any material, porous or not, including wood, acrylic, cork, Formica, and plastic | Adjustments cannot be made once the surfaces have been joined.<br><br>They are effective in joining large surfaces, although they are not suitable for end joints.<br><br>Useful for lining pieces of acrylic with wood veneer. |
| PVA glue | Suitable for joining wood, as well as for creating specific elements of the models, like green areas, or to fix areas of track ballast | Slow drying; adjustments can be made.<br><br>When applied to plastic surfaces (on green areas), these surfaces should be perfectly clean, otherwise craters will appear in the areas without adhesive, spoiling the work. |
| General observations: To get strong and reliable joins, the surfaces to which adhesives are applied should be free of paint, grease, dust, etc., otherwise the adhesive will bind to the layer of paint and will peel over time. It is also important to remember that the solvents in adhesives dissolve paints. | | Choose the most suitable adhesive for each particular process, taking into account its use and specifications, as well as the drying time. Such choices will depend on the glue's characteristics and on the environmental conditions of the workshop, as well as the possibility of making adjustments. |
| Request technical specifications and safety data sheets from the manufacturers. | | Specific adhesives are available for special applications that can be indicated for certain processes in modelmaking. Gather as much information as possible from the manufacturer, and make initial tests. |

# The base

◄ Design for the Tabakalera Building, Jon Montero, architect. Architectural model of acrylic veneered with laser-engraved sapele veneer, stainless-steel base, and interior lighting, made by Maquet-barna (scale 1:400), 2009. Winner of the international competition for the architectural renovation of the Taba-kalera Building in Donostia–San Sebastián, Spain.

Once the design has been studied, the preparatory work on the architectural model begins, starting with the base or stand. The base's size and characteristics will vary depending on each particular case, on the expressive and physical characteristics of the model, and on its scale and dimensions. To make a base, we have to take into account the size of the area that the model represents, the type of model, and its purpose, as well as its physical and material characteristics. The possible addition of a display case and eventual shipping should also be considered.

## Simple bases

Some types of models require a very basic stand or base. The process of fashioning a simple base made out of wood and then covering it with melamine veneer is shown here.

▲ 1. First, the dimensions of the base are established; to do this, a ½ in (1.5 cm) plywood board is cut to the required measurements, in this case 16 x 19 in (41 x 48 cm). Four 2 in (5 cm) wide battens of plywood of the same thickness are also cut; they are made somewhat longer than the sides of the previous piece. They are then attached to the base of the board with PVA glue and several tacks and left to dry. Finally, the excess parts of the battens are cut off with the saw, and the ends are polished with an electric polishing machine.

▶ 2. The base is covered with melamine. First, the pieces that will cover the sides are cut with a special cutter that allows the width of the cut to be adjusted and aligned.

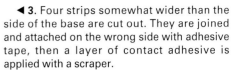

▶ 3. Four strips somewhat wider than the side of the base are cut out. They are joined and attached on the wrong side with adhesive tape, then a layer of contact adhesive is applied with a scraper.

▼ 4. A layer of adhesive is also applied to the sides of the base and allowed to dry for a few minutes. Shortly afterwards, when the glue is no longer tacky to the touch, a strip of melamine is placed on one of the sides. Tapping the piece with a hammer, using a block of wood to prevent the surface of the base from being marked, helps ensure that it is attached correctly. The other sides should be dealt with in the same way.

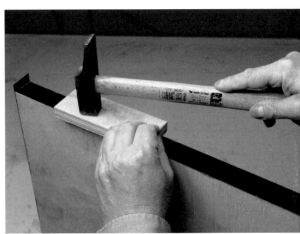

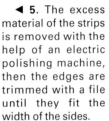

◀ 5. The excess material of the strips is removed with the help of an electric polishing machine, then the edges are trimmed with a file until they fit the width of the sides.

▶ 6. The veneer is now added to the top of the base. This is done by applying the melamine veneer in the same way as for the edges. However, to fix it into place, one of the sides should be arranged so that it is in contact with the edge of the base, and then trimmed like the page of a book.

▼ 7. The edges are trimmed with a file. The veneering of the base is now completed.

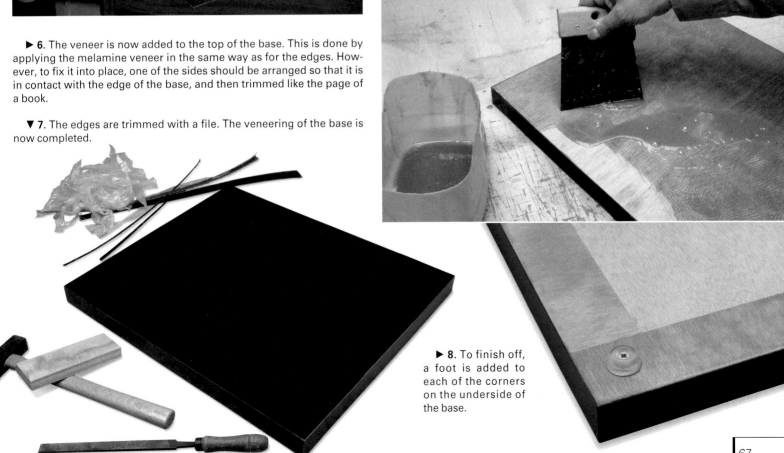

▶ 8. To finish off, a foot is added to each of the corners on the underside of the base.

# Veneering edges

To create simple bases or stands, you can use boards that are sold already veneered, cutting them to size according to needs, and finishing them off by veneering the edges to make a base that is similar to the previous example. Veneering the edges can also be done once the model is finished or while it is being made, depending on the circumstances. Both processes, which involve similar steps, are explained below.

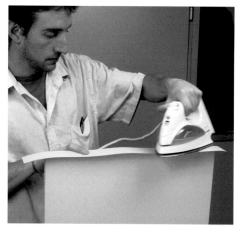

◄ **1.** Once the board has been chosen, the melamine veneer is attached. Here, a self-adhesive sheet is fixed into place by applying heat. A strip (see previous example) somewhat larger than the area to be veneered is cut out and positioned on the edge of the base. It is then attached by using a domestic iron set to the maximum temperature on the steam setting.

▲ **2.** The other sides of the base are dealt with in the same way. The excess veneer is then cut off with a utility knife, moving the knife from the outside in.

▲ **3.** To finish, a file is used to remove any rough edges from the veneer. The file is moved diagonally along the edge at a slight angle.

◄ **1.** Veneering the base of the model involves the same processes. The first step also consists of attaching the thermo-adhesive veneer with the help of a domestic iron.

▶ **2.** Cutting the excess veneer is always done from the wrong side, using a block of wood as a buffer to ensure a precise cut.

▶ ▶ **3.** Finally, the edges are trimmed with a file. They are always filed from the outside in and with the file somewhat inclined. This prevents scratching and marking the veneer, although any marks on the horizontal plane of the base will not be visible once it is painted or the covering applied.

# Thick bases

Thick bases are very common for architectural models. They are especially suitable for models of urban sites, as they allow specific elements—underground access points, slopes, etc.—to be created. It is essential to plan the position of the inner supports (ribs) of the base in advance, depending on the location of these elements in the model, as well as their specific characteristics.

▶ **1.** This example shows the creation of a base with a thickness of 2 in (5 cm) and large dimensions of 48 x 63 in (122 x 162.1 cm) using ¼ in (5 mm) MDF and 1 in (30 mm) chipboard. The first step consists of preparing the work surface on which the base is to be made, which should be sufficiently broad. The level is checked with a long metal ruler, and the two sides and diagonal measurement of the surface are verified.

▲ **2.** Once the boards that will make up the top and bottom of the base have been cut to the required size, a saw is used to cut the pieces of chipboard that will make up the sides of the base, with a width of 1½ in (4 cm).

▲ **3.** The length of the sides is measured and the cutting line marked on the pieces of chipboard that will make up the sides, leaving them somewhat longer. A portable electric saw is used to cut along the line.

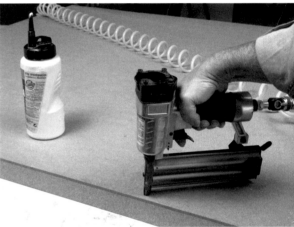

▲ **4.** A batten of chipboard is lined up with the outer edge of one of the boards, protruding beyond each of the ends. It is attached with PVA glue and a few tacks.

▲ **5.** Next, the batten is put into position on the other side so that it is also lined up with the edge of the board and meets the previous batten, protruding a little. This allows the work to progress rapidly and ensures that the sides fit correctly. This is also attached with PVA glue.

▲ **6.** Several tacks are nailed in to attach the batten to the board. A broad wooden block is positioned on the outside to stop the batten from moving during nailing and to ensure it is at right angles. The same is done with the remaining sides.

▲ **7.** The work is left to dry for 24 hours and the base is turned around. A screw is fixed into the central part of the join to ensure that the battens are secured into place and to prevent the joins from opening.

▶ **8.** Once all of the joins have been screwed into place, the inner ribs that will serve as a support for the top face of the base are made. The distance between the sides inside the base is measured and a batten with a similar width to the previous ones is cut from the chipboard. It is then glued down the center with PVA glue. The same procedure is followed to make and attach the two transverse battens (in a horizontal position in the picture). Glue is applied to the sides and the inner supports.

▲ **9.** The board that makes up the top of the base is carefully put into place and the glue is left to dry for 24 hours. Weights (such as heavy tools and pieces of machinery) are placed on top of the inner supports.

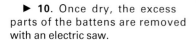

▶ **10.** Once dry, the excess parts of the battens are removed with an electric saw.

◀ **11.** Finally, the surface of the sides and the edges is sanded with an electric sander.

## Other bases

The use of nontraditional materials to create bases opens up a wide range of physical possibilities while offering new expressive resources for representation. Generally limited to competition models, these materials allow modelmakers to explore their skills and achieve innovative solutions. Here, the creation of the base for the architectural model illustrated in this section is shown.

◀ To create the model, designed to be shown at a competition, a base was made of ¹⁄₁₆ in (2 mm) stainless steel, and the pieces were joined with cyanoacrylate adhesive. This base includes the building's surroundings, with the underground access seen to the right of the picture. Openings needed to install lighting were left in the center.

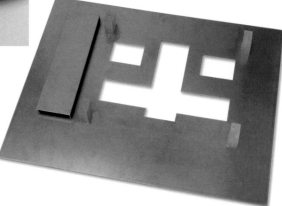

▶ View of the underside of the base. The bottom of the underground access is visible, as are the acrylic supports, also attached with cyanoacrylate adhesive. These supports separate the base from the bottom of the model where the interior lighting is to be installed.

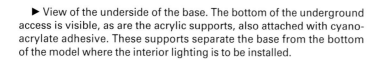

# Topographic representations

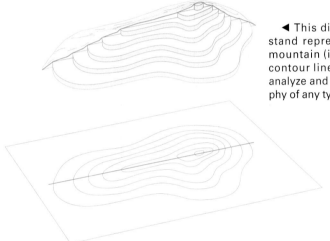

▲ Building project, Carlos Ferrater, architect. Architectural model of acrylic made by Maquet-barna on a pre-existing gypsum base with a topographic representation of the relief (scale 1:500), 1998.

◄ This diagram is an easy-to-understand representation of the relief of a mountain (in green) through the use of contour lines, by which it is possible to analyze and therefore model the topography of any type of terrain.

## Representation by strata

Topographical models reproduce the topography of a site, that is, the set of features presented by its surface configuration. It will have varying levels of detail depending on the scale and inherent characteristics of the architectural model, showing the relief and its specific characteristics. Topography is usually represented by using strata, layers, or levels based on the cartographical representation of the relief, made using contour lines. Contour lines can be used to depict in detail any relief in a site, for example, valleys, depressions (with discontinuous lines), mountains, hills, and inclines. Cartographical representations that use contour lines do not convey all elevations. They only depict those which correspond to certain altitudes that are defined on the basis of the scale of the representation, as well as the type of map. In these representations, lines are depicted according to a certain difference in altitude, known as equidistance. Therefore, on a topographical map or plan with an equidistance of, say, 100 ft or 100 m, only contour lines with elevations that are multiples of 100 will appear. The same applies in a representation with an equidistance of 50 ft (50 m), where the lines represented will be multiples of this number, starting from a certain elevation: 50, 100, 150, 200, and so on.

▼ **1.** In this case, the terrain relief will be represented topographically by strata made of white ⅛ in (3 mm) foam board. The model will be set on a preexisting base made in MDF. The first step consists of using reprographic techniques to reproduce the plan at the actual size of the model that is to be made and that will coincide with the dimensions of the base.

► **2.** The plan is placed on the base and the paper is cut, retracing the line of the first level curve with a utility knife.

► **3.** A wide fragment of foam board is cut out and lined up with the base. The plan is then lined up on the base and the contour of the line that was cut previously is marked in pencil. This will be the lower stratum of the model.

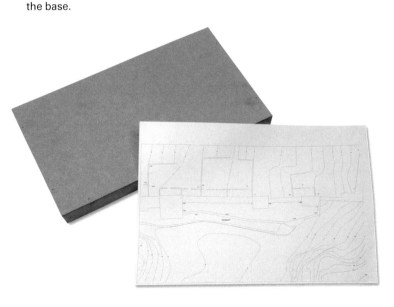

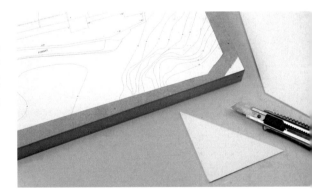

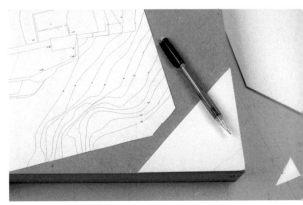

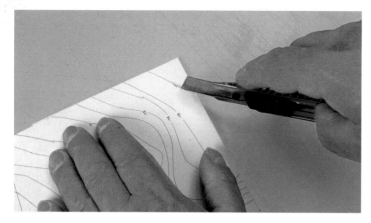

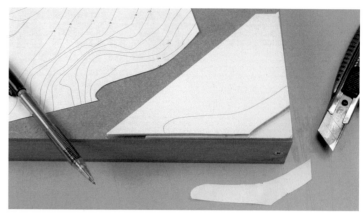

▲ 4. A similar fragment of foam board is cut out. The plan is lined up on this fragment and cut out following the cutting line of the first-level curve. The result is the first stratum of the model.

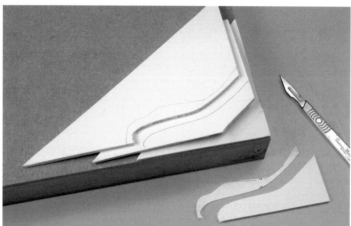

▲ 5. The same procedure is followed for the second stratum: the plan's second-level curve is cut out with a utility knife and marked on the piece of foam board in pencil.

◄ 6. The third-level curve is dealt with in the same way. The cutting line of the third stratum perfectly matches the contour of the level curve marked in pencil on the stratum below.

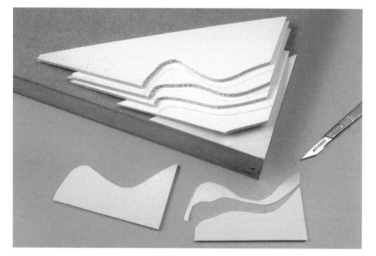

◄ 7. The fourth stratum is made.

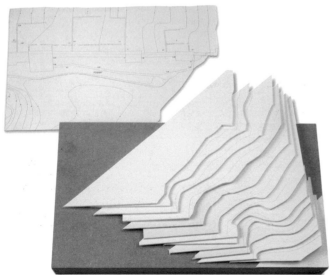

▲ 8. The work progresses, cutting out the plan where the contour lines are represented and making each of the strata. A scalpel is used to make very precise cuts like very sharp curves.

◄ 9. The strata are a perfect representation of the contour lines. If the model includes the representation of a building, the foam board is cut to include the outline of the building, as can be seen in the final stratum.

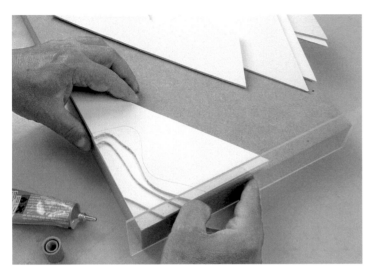

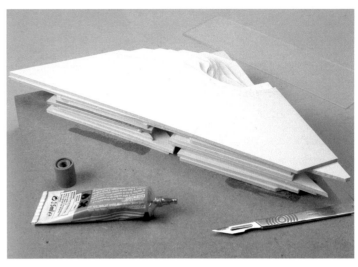

▲ **10.** The strata are then assembled; to do this, the edges of the pieces are carefully lined up on the base and attached with nitrocellulose adhesive. Here, a piece of acrylic is used to help prevent any irregularities during drying. It is held firmly with one hand while the other hand puts the strata in place.

▲ **11.** As the strata are overlapped, fragments of foam board are placed beneath to act as supports, and are joined with nitrocellulose adhesive.

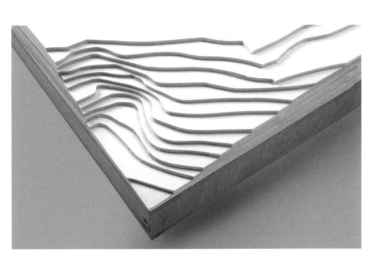

 ▶ **12.** The finished topographical representation.

## CONTOUR LINES

Contour lines are also called "isolines" (from the Greek prefix *iso*, which means "equal"). In cartography, they are the lines that join the points where they meet at the same altitude or elevation, in other words, at the same height above sea level. Contour lines are a convention used to clearly and easily represent the relief of a site, that is, the features on a site's surface, or its topography. Once the concept is understood, interpreting the representation of a site using contour lines is simple and should not present any problem. In a representation or plan that uses contour lines, lines very close to each other indicate a steep slope, as the altitude increases rapidly within a small horizontal space; in contrast, lines that are more spread out indicate a very gentle slope or flat area; a closed contour line without another inside it indicates a peak.

◀ For topographical representations in models with large dimensions, the use of polyurethane foam is recommended because it is lightweight and very strong. Here, it was used to create the strata of the topographical relief, as well as to make the supports.

# Representation by inclined planes

This method of representation consists of creating topography through the use of inclined planes or surfaces. It is used when we do not wish to offer a terraced image of the site (strata) in naturalistic representation models, where the topography and elements of the surroundings—vegetation, soil, water—are represented figuratively. Polyurethane foam is highly suitable for this due to its material characteristics in terms of weight and strength, as well as the fact that it is easy to work and can be used to make all kinds of planes.

▲ **1.** This shows the creation of a railway station bank in polyurethane foam. The project demonstrates the processes involved in making topographic representations using planes. Once the foam has been selected, a piece with dimensions somewhat greater than the area to be made is cut out. Here, the bank needs to fit perfectly alongside the building that protrudes beyond the top area of the site. It will therefore have to be cut according to the outline of the construction; its position is first marked with a pencil.

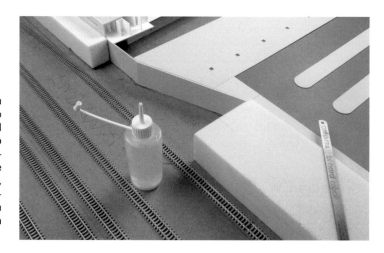

◄ **2.** The blade of a wood saw is used to cut along the pencil lines, checking to ensure that it fits perfectly. Note that the inside of the piece, which will be in contact with the top area of the site, has been marked with a cross.

▲ **3.** Following the outline of the top area of the site, a wall is made with two pieces of 1/16 in (2 mm) acrylic and fixed with acrylic glue, which helps create the bank and support the building that will be placed on top of it.

◄ **4.** The remaining pieces that will make up the bank are now cut out, first marking the inside with a cross to avoid any confusion.

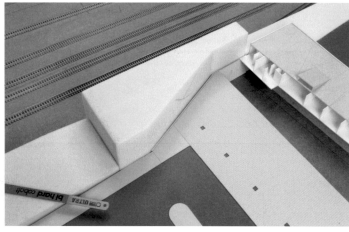

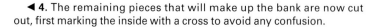

▶ **5.** Once the fit of the pieces has been checked, they are joined with contact adhesive. This is applied with a scraper to the two surfaces that are to be joined. When the surfaces are no longer tacky to the touch, the piece of foam is placed in the desired position. Care must be taken as this adhesive joins instantly so adjustments cannot be made.

▼ **6.** After all the pieces have been attached, work starts on the foam. The excess is first cut off with the blade of a wood saw; the blade is moved from the outside inward, making small, sideways sawing movements.

▼ **7.** The surface and the dimensions of the bank are given an even finish by smoothing with sandpaper.

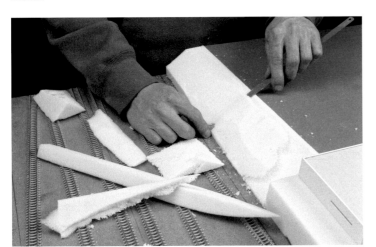

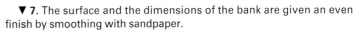

▶ **8.** The surface of the bank is sanded so that it is flush with the top and bottom areas of the site.

◀ Polyurethane foam can also be used to quickly and easily create undulating plans or reliefs.

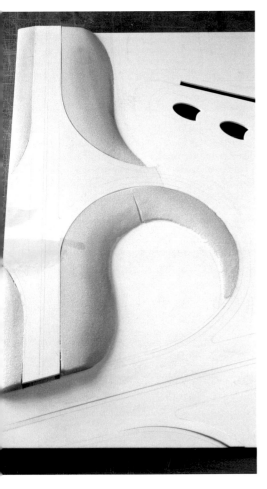

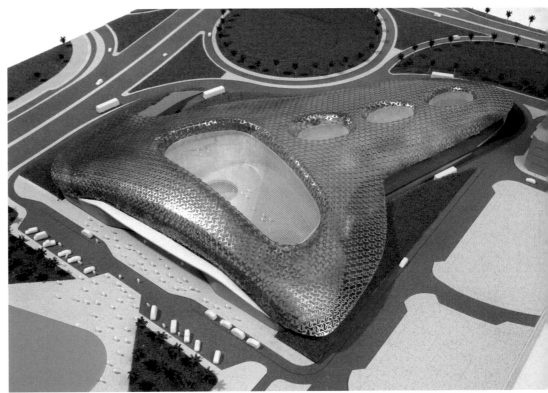

▶ The model finished. The undulating planes made of covered foam to represent vegetation can be seen in the background.

# Urban sites

Urban sites are considered a special case in topographic representations, although the way they are represented falls strictly within the sphere of building models: town planning, lay-out plans, and buildings with surroundings.

Nevertheless, topographic information such as differences in the elevation or relief of the site is included on urban sites. Other elements—roads, pavements, entrances, and under-ground ramps—are also included. The

creation of the road and pavements surrounding a block of homes is shown below, depicting the unevenness of the terrain.

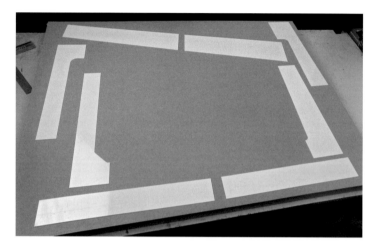

▲ **1.** Once the stand or base of the model is completed, the pieces that will make up the perimeter road of the block are made. They are laser-cut of ¹⁄₁₆ in (2 mm) acrylic following the design.

▲ **2.** The pieces are placed on the base in order to check that they fit together perfectly. They are then removed and set aside.

◄ **3.** The relief of the site, which has a gentle slope, comes next. Taking the design as guide, the side walls of the model are made. These will provide the support to the road on the site. They consist of four pieces of MDF cut to a determined width depending on the topographical elevations of the design: the first side goes from a width of 1 in (3 cm) at one end to 2 in (4.7 cm) at the other; the second varies from 2 to 3 in (4.7 to 7.8 cm) wide; the third, from 1 to 2 in (3 to 4.6 cm); and the last one from 2 to 3 in (4.6 to 7.8 cm). The four walls are put in place following the required lay-out without attaching them, and the wooden brackets are fixed with a tack and PVA glue.

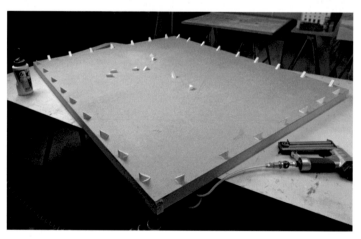

▲ **4.** The work is left to dry.

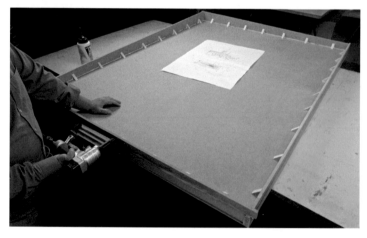

▲ **5.** Taking the plan as reference, the walls of the site are now put in place. They are attached to the underside with PVA glue and are nailed onto the wooden brackets with tacks. The work is left to dry. Note how the terrain slopes.

▼ **6.** To make the road, pieces of acrylic are fixed to the edge of the walls of the site. They are first arranged following the design and fixed provisionally with adhesive tape; later, a fine line of acrylic glue is applied to the upper edge of the wall.

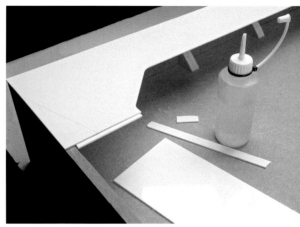

▲ **7.** The joins between the pieces of the road are made, using a piece of acrylic for support. Once one part of the road is fixed into place, acrylic glue is used to attach a narrow piece of ¹⁄₁₆ in (2 mm) acrylic to the next piece at the bottom of the join area.

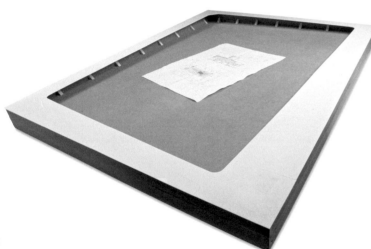

◄ **8.** A general view of the road once finished; the slope of the terrain can be seen on the front side.

▼ **9.** Roads are usually represented as asphalt-colored. To do this, they are first painted with a dark gray background. Here, another model with a base made in MDF is shown. Acrylic paint is applied with a roller in this example, although synthetic paint was used in the model that concerns us here. It is left to dry.

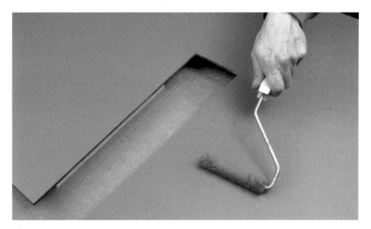

► **10.** To give a realistic effect that suggests the texture of the asphalt, a fine coat of light gray paint is applied using an airbrush; this gives a speckled effect.

► **11.** Once the paint is dry, the pavements are assembled. The picture shows a detail of the model with the completed road and the assembled pavements.

# Veneering

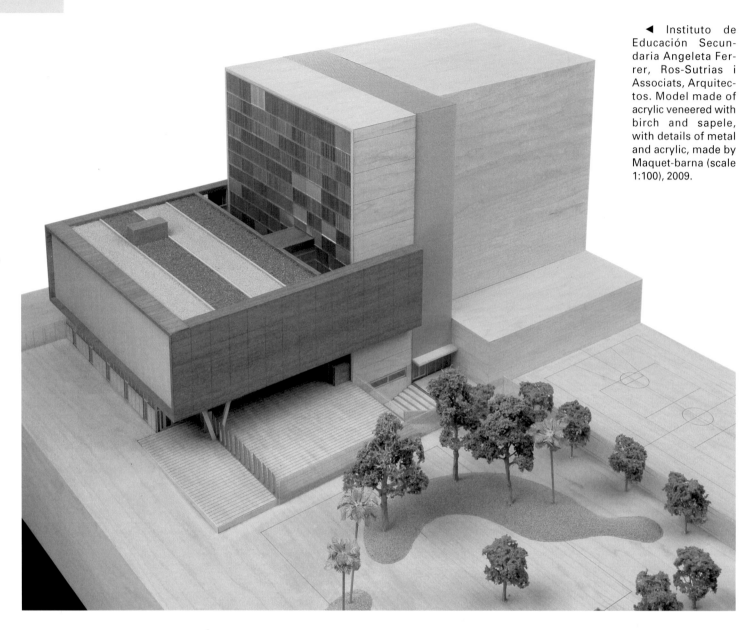

◀ Instituto de Educación Secundaria Angeleta Ferrer, Ros-Sutrias i Associats, Arquitectos. Model made of acrylic veneered with birch and sapele, with details of metal and acrylic, made by Maquet-barna (scale 1:100), 2009.

Veneering consists of covering a support with one or several wood veneers, which are attached to the surface with contact adhesive and pressed down firmly. The process requires that the support be prepared in advance, which involves sanding it down and making several grooves on the surface so that the wood adheres more easily. Any bumpiness or irregularities in the support will stand out once it is covered with the veneer and will therefore be noticeable.

Wood adds more expression to the model, which often translates into a higher-quality result. Furthermore, it offers a way of achieving interesting aesthetic effects based on alternating different types or grades of woods to highlight or personalize parts or elements of the model. The technique of veneering allows architectural models to be created where the wooden surface uses the acrylic as

a support. This speeds up the work, which can be done more efficiently than if only solid woods are used. It also affects the final cost, as some solid woods are very expensive

and veneers are more affordable. Once veneered, acrylic can be worked with a laser and cut without problems.

◀ 1. Once the piece of acrylic has been cut out and the veneer chosen, work can begin. A piece of veneer is cut which is slightly larger than that of the base and an even coat of glue is applied to the back. Here, a piece of acrylic will be veneered with two panels of birch.

► **3.** The surfaces covered with glue are left to dry until they are no longer tacky to the touch, and the panel is positioned according to the desired layout. This glue does not allow for last-minute adjustments. It is pressed down with a piece of wood (to avoid leaving marks on the panel), which is moved from the center outward following the direction of the grain of the wood.

▲ **4.** The second piece of panel is glued on, and the join or line where the two pieces meet is concealed by rubbing it with sandpaper following the grain of the wood.

▲ **6.** The piece once it has been veneered.

► **7.** Wood-veneered models are assembled in the same way as those made of acrylic. The parts are put together using the same glue; in this case, one specifically for acrylic.

◄ **2.** A coat of glue is also applied to the other side of the piece of acrylic, which has previously been sanded down, and on which some superficial crisscross lines have been scored with a utility knife.

▲ **5.** Next, the piece of acrylic is placed face down, with the wood paneling in contact with the work surface, and the excess paneling is removed with a utility knife.

# Making elements and coverings

Prefabricated elements are an important resource when making architectural models, because they enable you to work more rapidly; however, on many occasions it may be necessary to make certain items in the workshop so that they can be adapted to the measurements of a particular project. The processes used to create some of these elements are shown here; there are many more, depending on the type of model and its characteristics, but it would be impossible to cover them all here in full. General examples of some of the most common types will be shown, as well as other more specific types; the systems employed to make finishes using two different coverings are also explained.

## Staircases

Indoor and outdoor staircases are very common elements in architectural models. They are made out of steps: the piece that makes up each step is cut to the required width and with the length of two treads, in other words, twice the size of the step on which the foot rests; the riser, or the vertical plane of the step, will be that stipulated in the plans. The system used to create any kind of staircase is shown below. This procedure is also used to make spiral staircases.

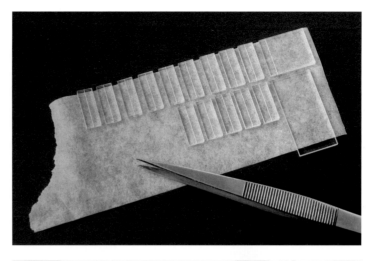

◄ **1.** This example shows how to make a staircase with two flights. First, all the pieces of acrylic are laser-cut. Note that a line has been etched on each piece. This will serve as a guide for assembly with the following piece.

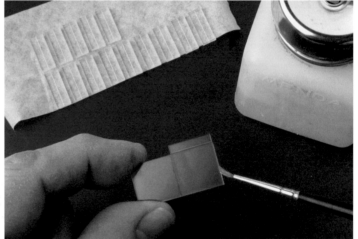

◄ **2.** The assembly is begun by joining the pieces which make up the double landing or central landing of the staircase with methylene chloride, which is applied to the joins with a fine brush.

▶ **3.** The two pieces that make up the landing are joined together using the etched lines for reference. Then the steps are assembled.

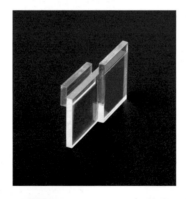

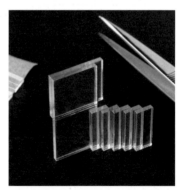

◄ **4.** First, one flight of stairs is attached; to do this, one of the edges is carefully lined up with the previously etched line.

▶ **5.** Next, the other flight is made up following the same process already described. Note that the resulting size of the steps is half the size of each piece.

▶ ▶ **6.** Now the banisters are made up and attached. The whole piece is fixed onto the work surface with double-sided tape to avoid any possible movement; then the banisters (made out of pieces of greenish-toned ¹⁄₆₄ in (0.5 mm) acrylic) are attached with methylene chloride.

# Interior furniture

### Seats and stools

The creation of different items of furniture is shown here. The production of the Barcelona chair and stool is explained first, following Ludwig Mies van der Rohe's original design for the German Pavilion at the 1929 Barcelona International Exhibition. These pieces are still produced today and sold in establishments specializing in designer furniture. The production of high bar stools is shown below.

◄ 1. The first step consists of cutting and engraving the pieces of white acrylic with the laser; here, the quilted effect of the upholstery of this furniture has been reproduced. Next, the pieces that form the back and seat of the chairs are joined with methylene chloride. These small pieces are handled with tweezers.

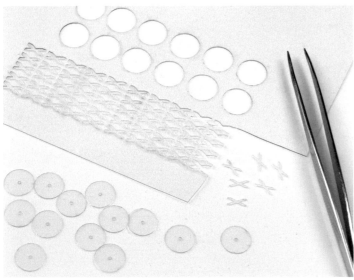

▲ 2. The legs of the seats and stools are cut from a piece of greenish-toned ¹⁄₆₄ in (0.5 mm) acrylic. The pieces that will form the tabletops are also cut (see below).

▲ 3. The pieces for the legs are spray-painted (see step 1 of the section on outdoor benches) and are attached with methylene chloride to the lower part of the seats and to the piece that represents the stools.

◄ 4. The high stools should have a wide upper base and another lower one of smaller dimensions, all made in clear ¹⁄₆₄ in (0.5 mm) acrylic, cut by laser. A polystyrene tube of ¹⁄₁₆ in (2.4 mm) diameter is attached to the centre of the wider base, while a similar tube of ¹⁄₃₂ in (1 mm) in diameter is fixed to the lower base. Finally, the upper part is spray-painted in white and the lower one in silver, and they are left to dry.

▼ 5. The stools are assembled using the tweezers, inserting the narrow tube inside the wider one.

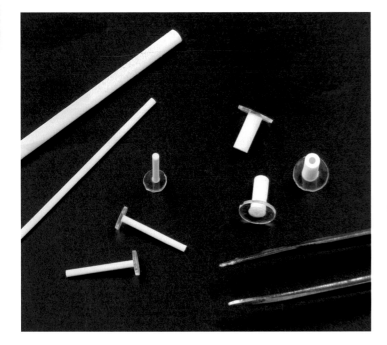

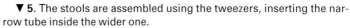

### Chair

The following example explains the process of making an office chair, originally manufactured in clear transparent polycarbonate with legs of chrome steel.

► **1.** To make up the seat, clear ¹⁄₆₄ in (0.5 mm) acrylic is used, engraved and cut by laser into square pieces of approximately ½ in (1.5 cm). To shape it, the acrylic is held with rubber-handled pliers and positioned on an insulating base made up of sheet polyester and mica, then heated with a heatgun on minimum settings for flow and temperature.

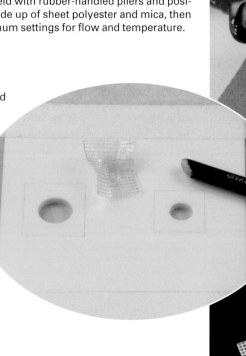

► **2.** Next, the piece is placed inside a mold made previously with leftover acrylic into which two ovals have been laser-cut. Various tests are carried out, and it is established that the most suitable one is the larger of the two. While still warm, the piece is placed over the larger oval and firm pressure is applied using a piece of wood (here, the cut end of a paintbrush).

► **3.** The result is pieces molded to look like the seat and back of the chair.

▼ **4.** The leftover material is cut away with the pliers to give an oval shape and the edge is polished with sandpaper.

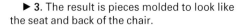

▼ **5.** Finally, the piece is attached with methylene chloride onto some preexisting legs. The result is chairs whose overall appearance resembles the originals.

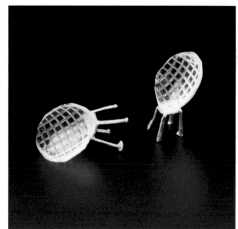

## Table

Similar processes are followed to make other elements, such as the table shown here. The pieces that make it up are cut out, painted, and assembled.

◄ The table is made from a base that has been pre-cut of ½ in (1 mm) acrylic, to which a polystyrene tube is attached with methylene chloride and which is then spray-painted silver. Once the base is dry, the top is attached (see step 2 of the section on seats and stools) with methylene chloride.

# Outdoor furniture elements

## Benches and chairs

The process of making outdoor benches and seats is shown next. These are a faithful representation of the originals, made of cast iron and wood. In this case, acrylic is used to make the piece that represents the arms and legs, and sapele wood veneer to represent the wooden parts.

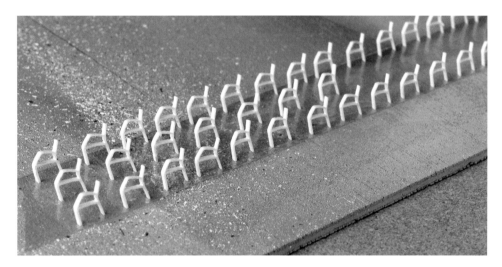

▲ 1. First, the piece used for the arms and legs is made, cutting it out of ⅓² in (1 mm) acrylic with the laser. It will constitute the side of the benches and chairs, and the seat and back will be fixed onto it. Next, the piece of wood panel is prepared. Both pieces are fixed onto a base (a scrap of wood) using double-sided tape.

◄ 2. They are then spray-painted with metallic gray paint and left to dry. The double-sided tape holds the pieces in place while the paint is being applied, and prevents them from falling and scattering.

► 3. The seats and backs are made out of panels of laser-cut sapele wood (to the right in the picture). They are attached to the side pieces using nitrocellulose adhesive, with the help of the tweezers.

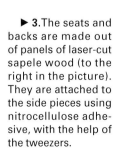

## Planters

It is also possible to create fixed outdoor furniture, either to hold plants, like planters or plant pots, or to separate or mark out spaces, like fences or walls. This example shows the creation of planters with grass that will then be used as a base for fixing trees.

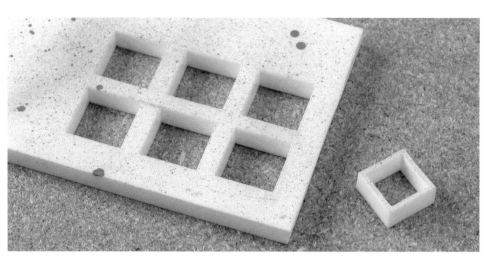

► **1.** The outer part of the planter is made of ¼ in (6 mm) acrylic, which is cut inside and out with the laser. Here, existing material with paint splotches is being reused.

◄ **2.** Following the process described in the previous section (benches and chairs), the exterior of the planter is spray-painted metallic silver. Then, a piece of polyurethane foam pre-cut to size is placed inside, and PVA glue is applied, to which ground grass representing the lawn is attached (see the section on covering green areas, page 91).

## Railings

These are typical elements in urban planning models. This example shows the creation of a railing with diagonal balusters and a straight handrail.

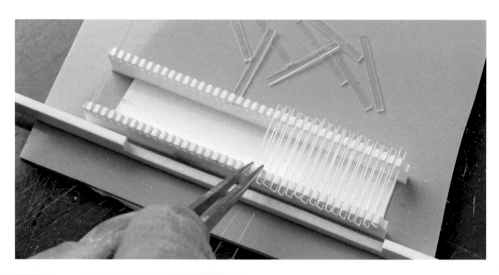

► **1.** A template is made on which to place the pieces that will form the balusters to ensure their correct diagonal positioning; here, it has been made out of two pieces of acrylic with diagonal indentations glued onto a base. The pieces for the balusters are cut out of ½₂ in (1 mm) acrylic and placed on the template with the help of the tweezers.

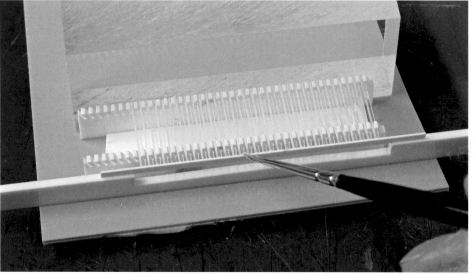

◄ **2.** The handrail is attached with methylene chloride. In order to avoid any possible irregularities in the balusters, a piece of acrylic is placed as a buffer at the back. Next, the piece which forms the handrail or banister is put in place, so that it is in contact with the ends of the pieces of the railings on a base (of pre-cut white acrylic) to support it, and it is attached with methylene chloride.

▲ **3.** A similar procedure is followed for the handrail or banister on the other side. View of various railings once assembled.

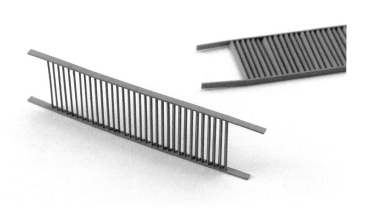

▲ **4.** Finally, they are spray-painted dark metallic gray.

# Windows

Windows are a key element of architectural models. The style used will depend on each particular case and the scale; they can range from very realistic, where the woodwork is shown in great detail with specific pieces, to abstract, with windows represented by a simple translucent enclosure. In general, the pieces that make up the windows are made somewhat larger than the opening they are intended to cover (some ⅟₁₆ in or 2 mm on each side), so that they can be attached correctly onto the back of the façade, although sometimes they need to fit the opening perfectly.

One of the ways of making windows that represent the woodwork is shown here.

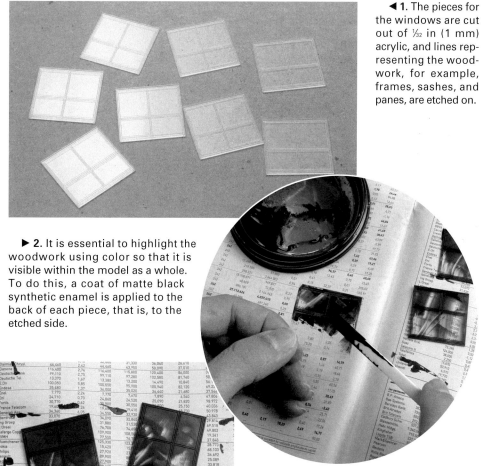

◄ **1.** The pieces for the windows are cut out of ⅟₃₂ in (1 mm) acrylic, and lines representing the woodwork, for example, frames, sashes, and panes, are etched on.

► **2.** It is essential to highlight the woodwork using color so that it is visible within the model as a whole. To do this, a coat of matte black synthetic enamel is applied to the back of each piece, that is, to the etched side.

◄ **3.** Before it dries, the excess enamel is removed with a clean cloth soaked in methylated spirit. The result is windows where the woodwork is visible.

# Roofs

Tiled roofs made up of inclined planes are another essential part of certain types of architectural model. Making them does not represent any real difficulty, as there is a wide choice of polystyrene sheets to choose from. The system used to create four-slope roofs (hip roofs) is explained in the example that follows.

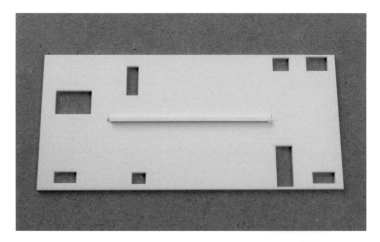

▶ **1.** First, the piece that will be used as the base for the roof is made. Here, a piece of ⅟₁₆ in (2 mm) acrylic has been cut following the existing plans. The plan shows that the roof will have chimneys; so, to act as a reference when cutting with the laser, apertures have been made in the base piece, although they will later be covered by the roof. The required gradient and dimensions of the gables are measured, and a piece of ⅟₁₆ in (2 mm) acrylic is cut out; the height will be that required to produce the inclination of the roof, and the length will be the same as that of the central ridge of the roof. It is then attached to the center of the piece with methylene chloride.

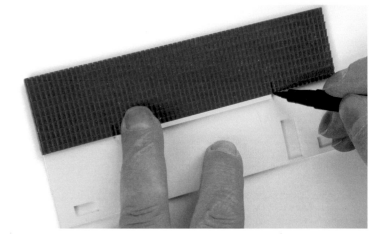

▲ **2.** The two main sides of the roof are made up; to do this, a piece of ⅟₁₆ in (2 mm) tiled polystyrene sheet is cut to the same length as the base piece, and just a little wider. It is put into the correct position and the location of the piece that defines the height is marked with permanent marker.

◀ **3.** The piece is now cut out, making a diagonal cut from the mark to the outer corner. The same procedure is followed with the piece for the other side. They are glued together with methylene chloride and then onto the base. All that remains are the other two slopes of the roof, which are made in the same way; the pieces are put in position and the place where the diagonal cut will be made is marked. If necessary, the edges can be altered with the polishing machine. They are attached with methylene chloride.

◀ **4.** One-slope roofs with access to a terrace are made from several pieces of polystyrene joined together with methylene chloride, and then finished off with roof edging.

▶ **5.** Detail of the edging on a one-slope roof.

# Areas of water and swimming pools

Representing areas of water will depend on the type of architectural model and its expressive needs; different materials and finishes can be used, depending on the requirements of the simulation. This can therefore be represented abstractly in conceptual models, as in the project for the port of Las Palmas de Gran Canaria (see page 18). A wide range of suitable materials is available, including vinyl sheets, card, and textured plastic or metallic sheets. In models that recreate natural features, acrylic is mainly used because its qualities allow effects of transparency and depth to be produced.

### Swimming pool

Special boxlike elements have to be made to create effects of depth. This example shows the creation of an outdoor swimming pool for an apartment building. The existing backing sheet on the acrylic is used to add color, because its blue is appropriate. However, a self-adhesive vinyl or plastic sheet, or a photo, could be substituted.

▲ Detail of a watercourse and pond from the architectural model of the monastery of Sant Llorenç prop Bagà and its surroundings as it was in the fifteenth century. The water has been depicted in a naturalistic way, to suit the representation and type of model (a historic reconstruction for educational purposes). It was made out of an acrylic base that was painted with different colors to imitate watercourses and ponds, and was covered with a sheet of clear shiny acrylic to recreate the transparency and brilliance of water.

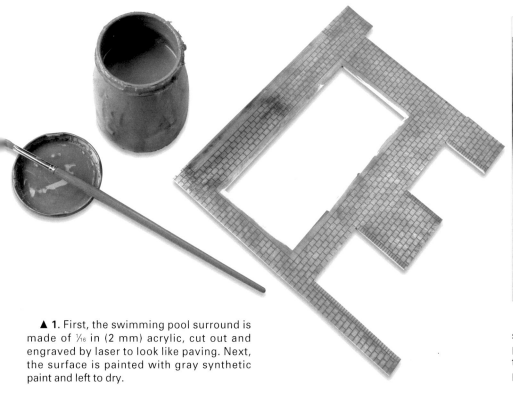

▲ **1.** First, the swimming pool surround is made of ¹⁄₁₆ in (2 mm) acrylic, cut out and engraved by laser to look like paving. Next, the surface is painted with gray synthetic paint and left to dry.

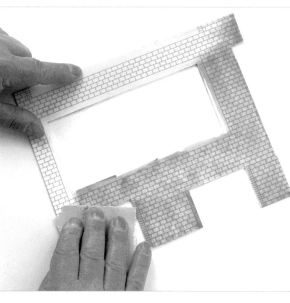

▲ **2.** The surface of the piece is rubbed with sandpaper to remove any excess paint, with paint only remaining within the etched lines; this provides an imitation of the original paving.

◄ **3.** The swimming pool tank is made of ¹⁄₁₆ in (2 mm) acrylic covered with a blue backing film. The pieces are cut with the saw.

▼ **4.** A piece of clear ⅛ in (3 mm) acrylic is used for the top part of the pool, representing the water. One of its surfaces is textured with wavelike forms. In the picture, all the pieces that make up the pool can be seen already cut.

► **5.** In order to glue the pieces together, the backing film must be removed from the area of the join, that is, a strip of between ¹⁄₁₆ to ⅛ in (2 to 3 mm) on each side. The film is also removed from the top piece (the water) of the pool.

▼ **6.** The side pieces of the tank are joined to the base of the pool and are secured with acrylic glue applied to the area that is free of backing film.

► **7.** The sides are joined as shown, leaving out one of the shorter sides. This is done to make sure that the sides of the pool fit together correctly.

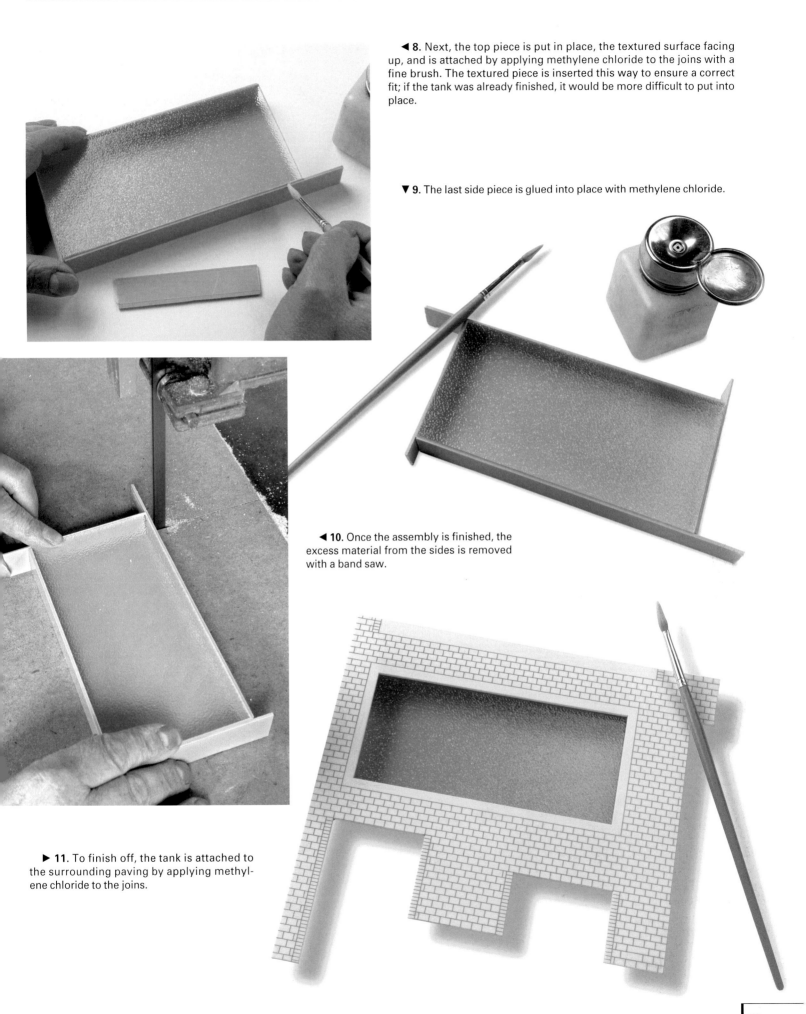

◀ **8.** Next, the top piece is put in place, the textured surface facing up, and is attached by applying methylene chloride to the joins with a fine brush. The textured piece is inserted this way to ensure a correct fit; if the tank was already finished, it would be more difficult to put into place.

▼ **9.** The last side piece is glued into place with methylene chloride.

◀ **10.** Once the assembly is finished, the excess material from the sides is removed with a band saw.

▶ **11.** To finish off, the tank is attached to the surrounding paving by applying methylene chloride to the joins.

# Coverings

### Track ballast

When creating presentation models of rail transport systems, the naturalistic representation of a specific element, called track ballast, is required. This is a layer of broken or crushed stone that is spread across the ground. The ties are placed on the ballast, and in turn the rails are laid and fastened on them; track ballast helps distribute the weight and stress caused by the trains. In architectural models, this is represented using gravel, which is sprinkled on once prefabricated tracks have been attached with PVA glue.

▲ 1. Once the model has been properly prepared and the surrounding elements (the main bank and the pieces that make up the platforms), have been protected, the gravel—a mixture of gray and white coarse gravel—is scattered over the surface to be covered.

◄ 2. The mixture is spread out evenly, and any gravel deposited on the tracks is removed with a coarse-haired brush.

▶ 3. The mixture is pressed down with a broad block of wood or any other resistant material until the surface is as smooth as possible.

▶ 4. To finish off, it is glued to the base and the particles of gravel are glued together with PVA glue previously dissolved in water in a proportion of 3 parts water to 1 glue (a ratio of 3:1). The first coat is applied with an airbrush or atomizer and is left to dry. Afterwards, it is given a couple more coats and left to dry until it is all perfectly glued together.

## Green areas

One of the most common elements in terrain, layout, and urban planning presentation models are green areas and vegetation. How they are represented varies depending on the type of model and its expressive needs; as in the case of water, a wide range of materials and resources can be used. They can either be represented schematically in conceptual models, as in the project for the port at Mataró (see page 16), using areas in different shades and colors and with sponge dyed green to represent the trees, or in a totally naturalistic fashion, as in the architectural model of the Iberian settlement at Turó de Montgrós in El Brull (see page 20).

Green lawn areas are often represented in architectural models. Two ways of making lawns are shown below.

▼ 1. The first step is to apply a fixative. Green acrylic paint is used, which is easily applied to the acrylic; the result is an even coat, without holes or bubbles, which provides the background color. The paint should have a thick consistency, not too liquid, with enough body that the grass will adhere to it. Once it has been applied, the grass is generously spread out over the still wet paint, and is pressed down firmly using both hands. Fingermarks can be seen in the picture.

◄ 2. Once the paint is dry, any excess can be recovered with a clean paintbrush and collected in a piece of paper.

▼ 3. View of the green area finished.

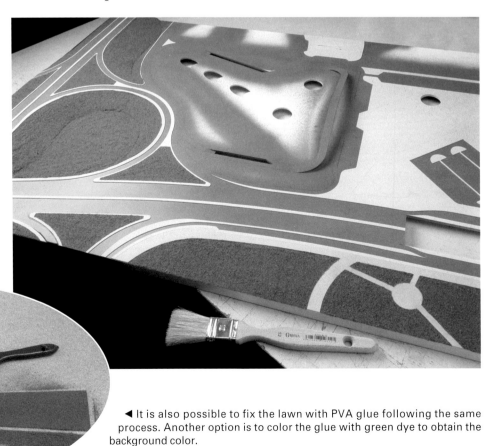

◄ It is also possible to fix the lawn with PVA glue following the same process. Another option is to color the glue with green dye to obtain the background color.

# Lighting

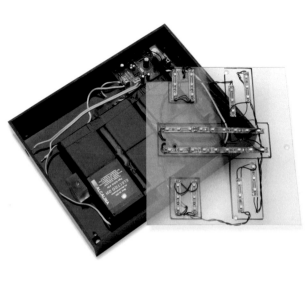

Lighting is an important feature of architectural models, given its inherent possibilities for expression. It may be just another element of the model or can become a fundamental aspect. Used exclusively in presentation models and mainly in models made of acrylic, lighting brings added interest to the representation and allows innovative aspects to be explored.

Lighting can be used to highlight the inherent values of the architecture represented, as well as to draw attention to or emphasize parts of the model, making it a first-class resource for conceptual models. It can be used too to represent the original lighting of the building or an interior. Lighting systems depend on each particular model, as well as on the effects we wish to achieve. In each case, the most suitable system will be chosen according to the type of model, its purpose, and the materials used.

◄ View of the installation of a lighting system inside the base of an architectural model. It consists of LEDs attached to the top part of the base, powered by a six-cell battery placed inside the base. The installation was completed with a switch so the lights in the model can be switched on, and a timer, which regulates the disconnection.

▲ Theater-auditorium in Esplugues de Llobregat, Barcelona, designed by Ramon Sanabria Arquitectes Associats, S.L. Architectural model of acrylic made by Maquet-barna (scale 1:100), 2003. Architectural model of the interior section of the building where the effect created by the lighting in the different spaces can be seen. On the top floor, the lighting of foyer and passageways has been resolved using LEDs to suggest the points of light in the design. The back wall of the lower floor of the model was made of transparent acrylic and was back-lit with a fluorescent tube to create all-round lighting.

► Apartment building in Barcelona, Carlos Ferrater, architect. Architectural model of acrylic made by Maquet-barna (scale 1:100), 2003. General architectural model of the building in which very well thought out interior lighting, made using various resources, highlights the individual style of the architecture, showing the naturalistic lighting of the different apartments.

The final stage in making architectural models consists of protecting and packing them. Normally, a display case to protect the model is essential and indeed unavoidable. Of course, packing is also necessary when the model has to be shipped.

## Display cases

Display cases are an effective way of protecting architectural models, and in turn allowing the models to be viewed. They guard the work, which is inherently fragile and delicate due to its material and physical characteristics, and keep it out of reach of viewers. This prevents any damage caused by human activity or external agents, including dust. The cases can be made of glass or acrylic, but the latter is preferable due to its light weight, which makes it easy to handle and place over the model, and because it does not make the piece much heavier. In addition, acrylic has similar characteristics to glass, with its strength, transparency, and shine. The greatest inconvenience is that it is easily scratched, which has to be taken into account for exhibition models.

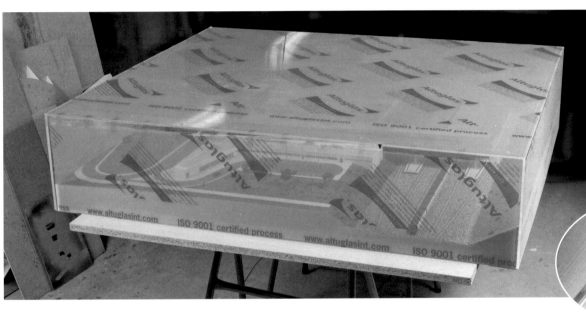

◀ Once an architectural model is completed, it must be protected by an acrylic display case. The display case is put in place, and the plastic backing film is removed to prevent any possible scratches during handling.

▶ To fix the display case into place, secure the corners with a piece of steel screwed into the underside of the base of the model, slightly protruding; the corner of the showcase rests on this. Note that a stopper has been put in place as a foot.

▲ A piece of steel with curved outer edges can also be used, which allows for some slight variation in the positioning of the display case, preventing any unevenness. This display case is lit, and a gap has therefore been cut into the side so that it can be connected to an electric outlet.

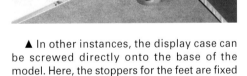

▲ In other instances, the display case can be screwed directly onto the base of the model. Here, the stoppers for the feet are fixed to the underside of the base.

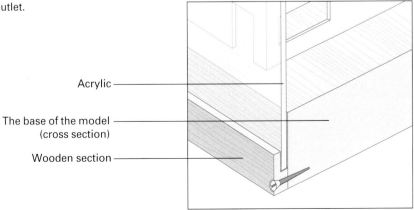

Acrylic ———

The base of the model ——— (cross section)

Wooden section ———

▲ It is also possible to position the display case by resting it on the base of the model, to which a batten has previously been glued, acting as a support.

◀ A made-to-measure frame can even be made for the display case once it has been placed over the model to ensure that it fits properly. A piece like the one in the illustration is made, and screwed onto the side of the base.

# Boxes

When a model has to be shipped, a special packing case must be made which conforms to the model's measurements and needs. It must be strong and reliable, designed to guarantee the integrity of the piece during handling, storage, and shipping, and to ensure that it reaches its destination in perfect condition. The production of a portable packing case for an architectural model is shown below.

▲ **1.** ¼ in (5mm) medium-density fiberboard (MDF) is used to make the top part and ⅜ in (10 mm) MDF is used for the sides.

◄ **2.** The box is fixed to the base of the model, which will also act as the bottom of the piece. The base of the model is therefore used as a guide while building it. To do this, the side pieces are placed by the sides of the base and attached with PVA glue; next, the upper part is glued and the work is left to dry. The box is now guaranteed to fit the base of the model. Here, the pieces were cut to slightly larger dimensions than those required, simplifying the work.

► **3.** Excess material is removed with an electric polishing machine.

◄ **4.** The edges are bevelled with an electric planer.

► **5.** The box is screwed onto the base of the model. The position of the screws is measured and marked with a pencil, and the hole where they are to be inserted is made; the MDF is reduced with a reamer so that the screws fit correctly.

◄ **6.** To protect the top of the model, polyurethane foam made specifically for packaging is fixed with double-sided tape to the top of the inside of the box. In other cases, it may be necessary to fully line the interior.

▲ **7.** Lastly, the box is screwed onto the base. Note that the box rests on a batten which allows for its position to be adjusted on the base.

◄ In other cases, it may be necessary to make a box into which the whole model is placed, which is then covered with a screw-down lid. To place the model inside the box, a wide piece of braided plastic tape is used, such as that used for roller blinds. The tape is passed underneath the base of the model, which can now easily be lifted. Afterwards, the model is carefully lowered into the box, which is positioned on the floor very close by. If necessary, packaging foam can be added.

▲ The boxes should also be fitted with reinforced corners on the base, and with strong, reliable handles to allow for easy handling.

▲ Interior view of the handles showing how they are attached.

*T*his section, a step-by-step guide to the process of creating a series of architectural models, consists of five projects in which the different phases of the work are described, from original design through completion. Different technical aspects and work systems are shown for each project, highlighting the wide variety and versatility of this discipline, as well as the many solutions that can be used. All the step-by-step guides have a clear didactic purpose, and are therefore complemented by explanations of the physical and technical resources used in each case. The aim is not to offer mere examples for readers to copy, but rather to serve as a guide to all the phases involved in the work and to show the resources needed at each stage.

# Step-by-step guide

# Cultural center

The first step-by-step guide explains the entire process involved in creating the architectural model for an original design by architect Carlos Ferrater for a competition for a cultural center in Lanzarote (one of the Canary Islands). Made by Pere Pedrero, this model is a massing presentation, intended to show the general forms and masses of the architectural project. It is made out of blocks of acrylic of different thicknesses that have been given a translucent effect, positioned on a base of aluminum sheet covered with green-toned acrylic that suggests the building's surroundings. Although this does not involve any excessively complex processes, it does require the use of special machinery and skill in cutting plastic and metal.

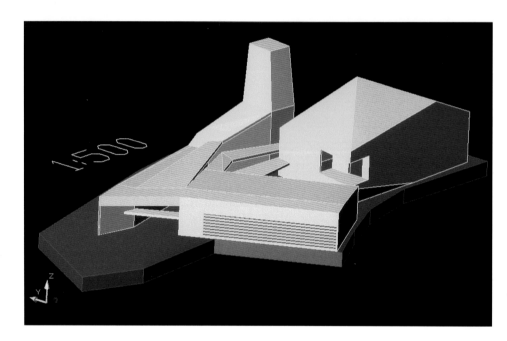

◄ **1.** An architectural model is made to a scale of 1:500 from an original design by Carlos Ferrater. The picture shows the massing design of the building and its surroundings.

▼ **2.** The floor plans and the four side elevations will be needed to make the model. The modelmaker uses these as a template to make the piece that represents the surroundings, and to put the masses of the building into place, as well as for reference during the different stages of the job.

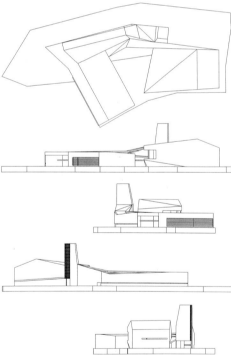

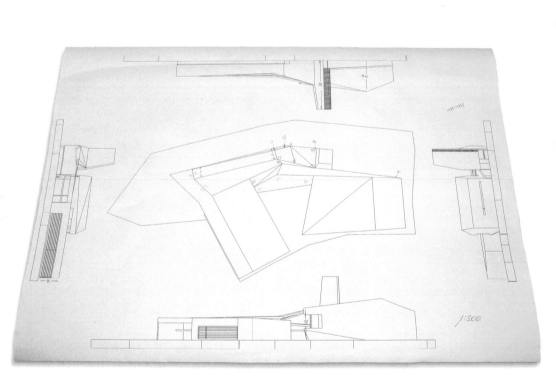

◄ **3.** The plan is reproduced to the actual size of the model, and a copy is made. In the first phase of work, this copy will act as a template for cutting the pieces of acrylic that make up the building, and the actual size plan (pictured) will be used as a guide for positioning the masses once cut.

▲ **4.** The perimeter of the building's ground plan is cut out on the copy, followed by the blocks that form the masses, which will be used as cutting templates. Various pieces of clear acrylic are chosen for the blocks, in this case, with a thickness of ½, 1, 1¼, 1½, and 2 in (12, 25, 30, 40, and 50 mm). The template for each block is placed over the corresponding piece (the picture shows one of 1¼ in [30 mm] thickness), and is attached using two small pieces of double-sided tape.

▲ **5.** The acrylic is cut using a band saw, making sure that the blade follows the edge of the template. It should not be cut too quickly, as acrylic heats up with friction and tends to stick to the blade of the saw. This could cause defects in the cut, giving ragged edges that are not perfectly straight.

▶ **6.** As they are cut, the pieces are placed on the actual size plan, positioning them as indicated.

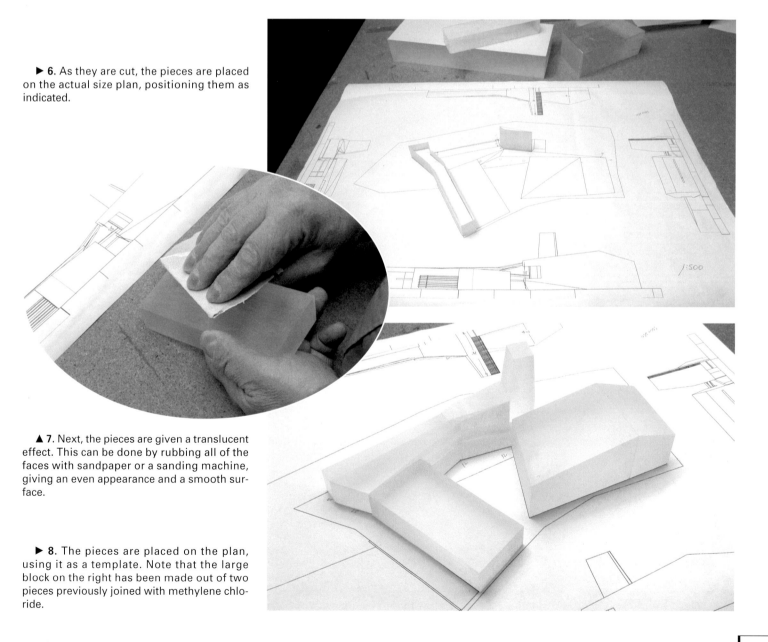

▲ **7.** Next, the pieces are given a translucent effect. This can be done by rubbing all of the faces with sandpaper or a sanding machine, giving an even appearance and a smooth surface.

▶ **8.** The pieces are placed on the plan, using it as a template. Note that the large block on the right has been made out of two pieces previously joined with methylene chloride.

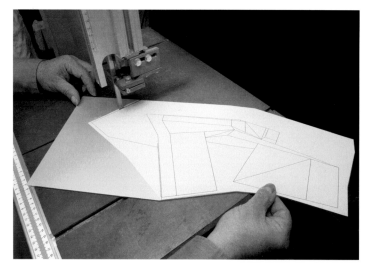

▲ 9. Once the pieces are finished, the base that will make up the surroundings of the project must be made. To do this, another copy of the plan is made to actual size and the perimeter cut out. It is then fixed onto ¹⁄₁₆ in (2 mm) aluminum sheet with two small pieces of double-sided tape. A saw equipped with a blade for metal can be used for cutting.

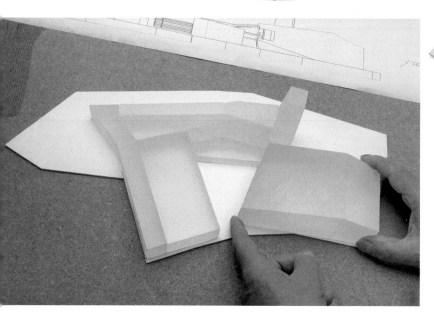

▲ ▲ 10. The aluminum is cut out carefully, using straight lines, following the lines of the template; cutting continues to the edge of the sheet and excess material is removed. Care must be taken not to go beyond the lines of the template inside the shape.

◄ 11. The outlines of the pieces have been adjusted and the edges polished with the polishing machine.

▲ 12. The result is a piece of aluminum that is the same shape as the base of the design and that has the same dimensions as the template.

◄ 13. Using the template as a guide and the plan for reference, the blocks are positioned following the layout of the design, and a check is made to ensure that they fit together correctly. At this point, if necessary, the dimensions of the pieces can be adjusted by cutting or retouching until they fit perfectly with one another and on the template.

▶ **14.** The template is removed carefully from the piece of aluminum. Using the plan for reference, a piece of greenish-toned transparent acrylic slightly bigger than the aluminum is cut out. It is fixed onto the aluminum piece with two small lengths of double-sided tape.

▼ **15.** The edges of the acrylic are trimmed with the polishing machine to make it the same size as the lower aluminum base. Next, the two pieces are carefully separated and the glue removed with alcohol; the backing film is also removed from the acrylic.

▶ **16.** The area where the acrylic blocks will later be placed is covered with silver-colored vinyl. To do this, the paper template is placed on the work surface, and the piece of greenish-toned acrylic is placed carefully over it. The surface of the acrylic is cleaned to remove any dust and dirt, and soapy water is applied with an atomizer. To ensure that the vinyl will adhere, excess water and any bubbles are removed by pressing down firmly with a scraper from the center to the edges of the piece. It is left to dry.

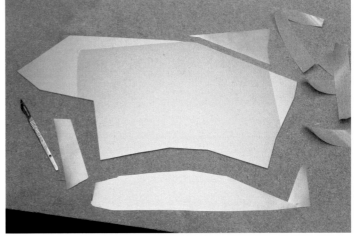

▲ **17.** The template is placed centrally over the piece of aluminum and the central part is cut away with a scalpel, giving an area slightly smaller than the zone where the acrylic blocks will be placed. Double-sided tape is placed over the area.

▲ **18.** The backing paper is removed from the double-sided tape and the piece of acrylic is carefully attached, in such a way that its edges coincide with the piece below. Pressure is applied to make sure that the pieces adhere, then the excess vinyl is removed with a scalpel.

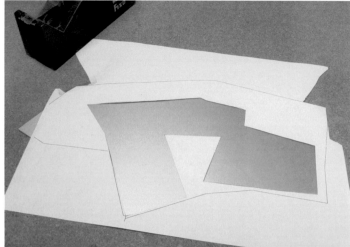

◀ **19.** Next, the blocks of acrylic that make up the built area are attached. To do this, the template is positioned centrally over the piece that makes up the base, and it is fixed onto the work surface with adhesive tape to avoid any movement. Note that cuts have been made in two corners of the template as an aid to correct positioning.

▲ **20.** Using the original plan as a guide, the pieces of acrylic are attached to the surface of the base with double-sided tape so that they coincide with the template.

◀ **21.** The excess vinyl is cut away with a scalpel, making sure that no marks are left on the upper acrylic surface of the base.

▲ **22.** The finished piece.

◀ **23.** A stand measuring 16 x 19 in (41 x 48 cm) wide and ½ in (1.5 cm) high is made out of wood with a Formica veneer (see pages 66–67).

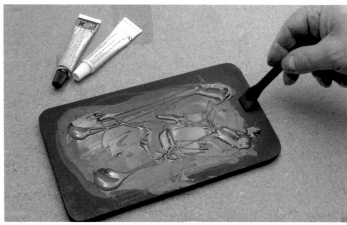

▲ **24**. The aim is for the model to be raised somewhat above the stand, as if suspended over it. To achieve this effect, an intermediate support piece that is smaller than the base is needed. A piece of ⅜ in (1 cm) medium-density board is cut to measure 5 x 8 in (12 x 20 cm) on all four sides, and this is spray-painted black with bodywork paint.

▲ **25**. The piece is fixed onto the center of the stand using two-part adhesive.

◀ **26**. The position of the model is measured and marked on the stand with drafting tape. The model is glued onto the intermediate support, also using two-part adhesive.

▼ **27**. The finished model.

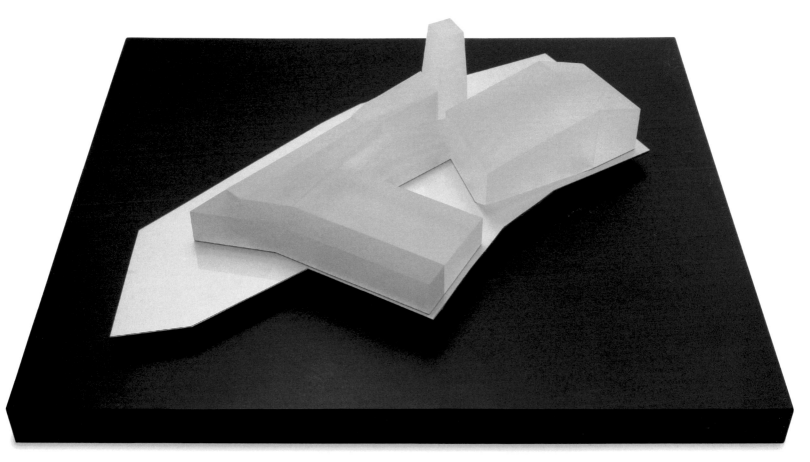

# Apartment building

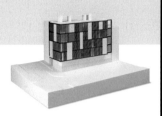

The following example shows the process involved in creating the architectural model for an apartment building according to the original design of architect Albert Brito. The model, made by Toni Martín, consists of a building located on a corner, between dividing walls, with a main façade that looks out over the street with balconies and slatted blinds, and a second, rear façade. The model combines the representation of the building's structure with the surfaces defined by the slatted blinds. It is built floor by floor, then the covering of the façade is added, in this case the blinds. The aim here is to represent the rhythm of the masses of the building's main façade and the interplay of chiaroscuros offered by the slatted blinds, as well as transmitting a diaphanous effect for the rooms located at both ends of the building. In addition, the roads that surround the building are represented as masses, as are the surrounding buildings.

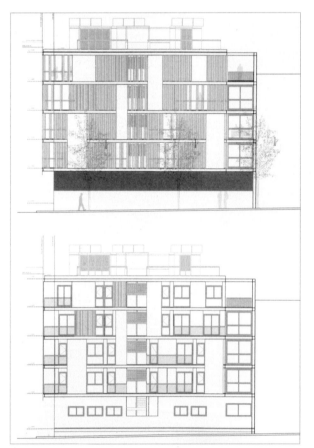

◄ ▲ 1. Plans of the front and side elevations of the building showing the façades, with their enclosures and balconies, in which the large sitting-room windows are a particular feature. The positioning of the slatted blinds is also visible.

▼ ▼ 2. Computer graphic images showing two views of the building, where the features of the construction can be seen clearly. The model was made to a scale of 1:75.

▶ **3.** The base is made first, using a piece of chipboard measuring 2 x 16 x 12 in (5 x 40 x 30 cm)—see pages 69–70. Next, the roads and the pieces for the pavements are made of 1⁄16 in (2 mm) acrylic cut by laser.

▶ **4.** The slope of one of the streets is also made, following the plans. To prevent the acrylic that makes up the pavement from sagging, a supporting piece is inserted between it and the base.

▶ **5.** Using the plans for reference, the lower part of the structure is made along with the building´s entrance hall (see the computer graphic image of the side façade in step 2).

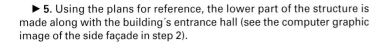

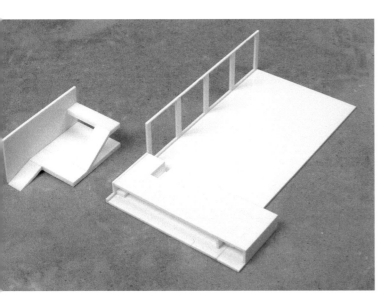

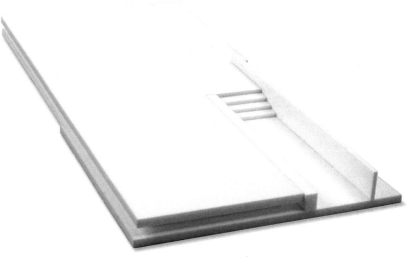

◀ **6.** The lower part of the staircase, which connects the corridor to the bottom of the stairwell, and one of the side façades are made of 1⁄16 in (2 mm) acrylic.

▶ **7.** Next, each of the building's four floors is made of 1⁄8 in (4 mm) acrylic. The outer walls are cut out of 1⁄16 in (2 mm) acrylic, and glued with methylene chloride. To ensure that they are correctly glued and to avoid any shifting, the windows, made of 1⁄16 in (2 mm) translucent acrylic, are also glued in the same way; this ensures that the model fits together.

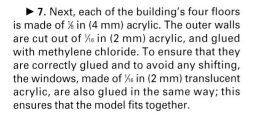

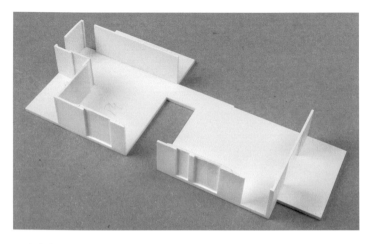

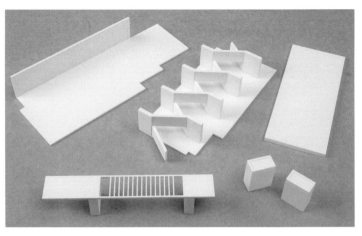

▲ **8.** Next, the window pieces are protected with drafting tape, and painted synthetic white using a spray gun (the picture shows the top floor).

▲ **9.** The pieces that will make up the staircase, of ⅛ and ³⁄₁₆ in ¹⁄₆₄ in (3 and 4 mm) acrylic, the rear façade and the pieces for the roof, both of ¹⁄₁₆ in (2 mm) acrylic, are now made and painted in the same way.

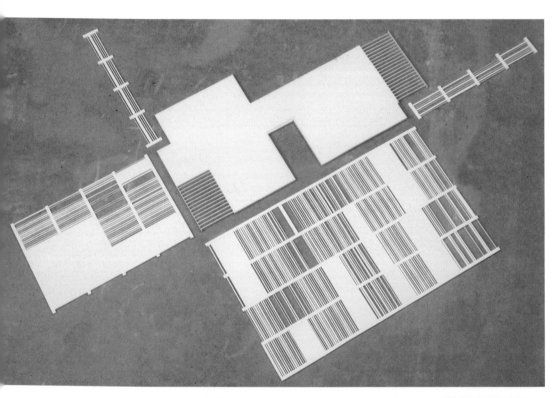

◄ **10.** Finally, the pieces for the slatted blinds at the front and sides of the building are cut out of ¹⁄₁₆ in (2 mm) acrylic and the roof pieces are cut out of ³⁄₁₆ in (4 mm) acrylic.

▼ **11.** Assembly of the model begins by joining the side walls of the lower part of the building to the piece below this, as well as to one of the side walls, specifically the right-hand dividing wall. They are painted white (following the instructions already described). Once dry, the piece is protected, except for the lower part, using paper and drafting tape as masks, and it is painted with a spray gun to give a speckled grayish effect.

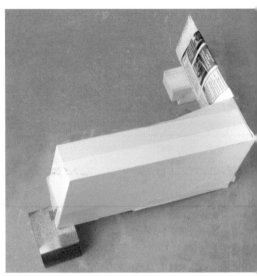

◄ **12.** New masks are placed over the area that has already been painted, removing those which cover the two vertical parts, and they are spray-painted gun metal gray. Next, the first floor of the building is assembled. To ensure correct positioning, supports are made out of ³⁄₁₆ in (4 mm) bars of acrylic and attached with methylene chloride.

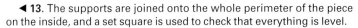

◄ **13.** The supports are joined onto the whole perimeter of the piece on the inside, and a set square is used to check that everything is level.

▼ **14.** The lower part of the building once assembled. Note the supports on the inside.

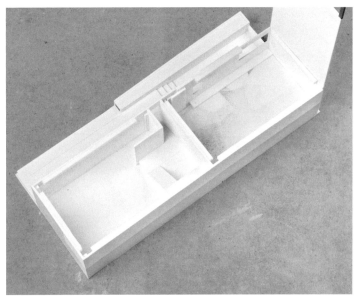

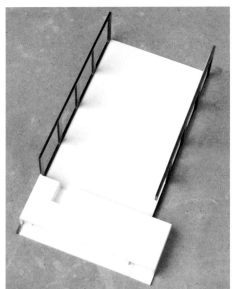

◄ **15.** The side façade is painted white and left to dry. Next, after protecting the rest with paper and drafting tape, the part of the façade that will have windows is painted with metallic spray paint. It is left to dry and the other side is glued, as with the first, with methylene chloride. The coat of paint around the area to which the glue will be applied must first be removed so that the pieces adhere properly.

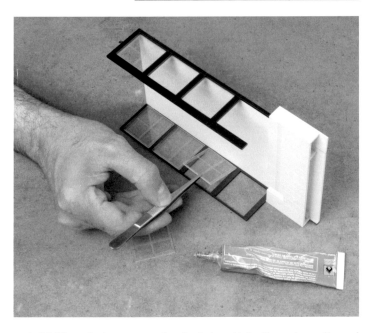

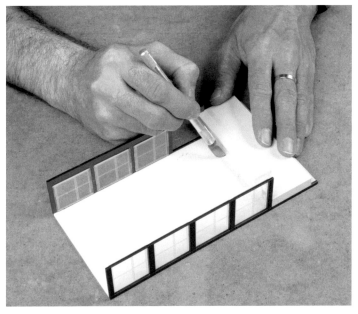

▲ **16.** The windows are cut out of clear ¹⁄₃₂ in (1 mm) acrylic and engraved. They are glued with nitrocellulose adhesive. The large lower window of the top side is not attached, as this is a door that needs to be fitted into the first floor of the building; if it was put in place at this point it could cause problems later.

▲ **17.** Next, the side façade is joined to the first floor of the building; to do this, the coat of paint on the area to be joined is removed with a scalpel, otherwise the methylene chloride would run off the paint and prevent the pieces from adhering.

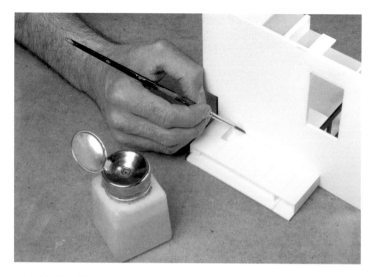

▲ 18. The first floor is attached to the side façade with methylene chloride, using a fine brush. The glue is applied to the front and back of the joins.

▲ 19. The whole ensemble is joined to the lower part of the building with acrylic glue.

▶ 20. The piece is positioned carefully over the ensemble and pressure is applied to fix it into place.

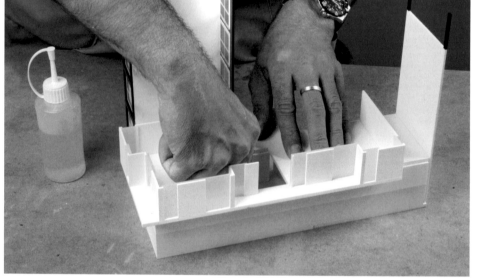

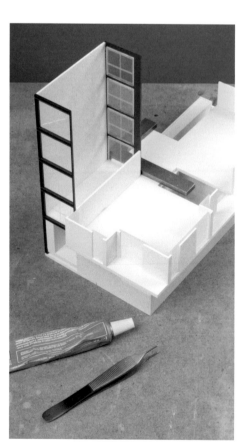

◀ 21. Lastly, the lower door is placed below the three large side windows and glued into place with nitrocellulose adhesive. A set square is used to check that it is all level.

▶ 22. The remaining floors are assembled using acrylic glue, paying particular attention to their order (having previously made pencil marks on the inside to show the position of each one—see step 8).

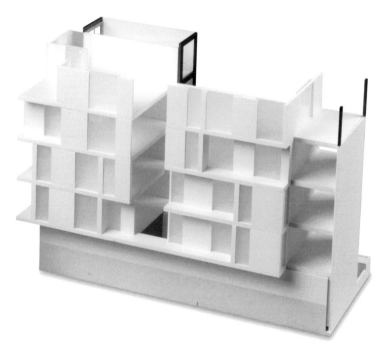

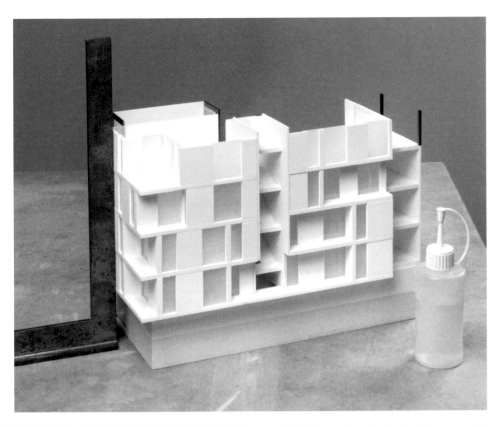

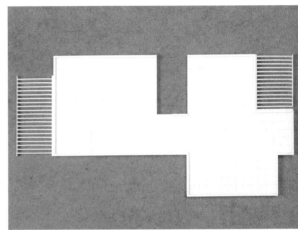

◀ **23**. A set square is used to check that the façades are perfectly aligned.

▼ **24**. The small perimeter railings of the roof are put into place by gluing on $\frac{1}{16}$ in (1.5 x 2 mm) polystyrene strips with methylene chloride. They are painted white and left to dry.

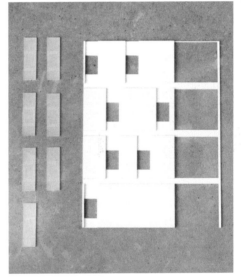

◀ **25**. The roof is glued onto the ensemble with acrylic glue; to do this, it is held with a plastic clamp and a weight is placed on top. To prevent the weight from leaving a mark on the surface of the model, a piece of wood is inserted between them. Two strips of acrylic are placed on the lower part of the façade and glued on with a drop of methylene chloride; they will act as a guide for the subsequent assembly of the façade.

▶ **26**. The piece which forms the rear façade of the building is also cut out of $\frac{1}{16}$ in (2 mm) acrylic, as well as the engraved pieces which stand out, and they are attached with acrylic glue. The windows are cut out of transparent $\frac{1}{16}$ in (2 mm) acrylic and engraved.

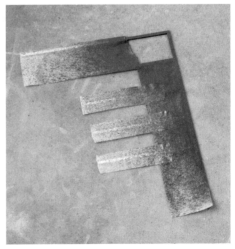

▶ ▶ **27**. The piece which will finish off the façade positioned between the floors is cut out and sprayed with dark gray metallic paint. Note that drafting tape has been use to mask out areas on both sides, so that only the areas that will be visible are painted, and not those which will be glued onto the model.

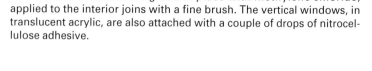
**28.** The windows are glued in place with methylene chloride, applied to the interior joins with a fine brush. The vertical windows, in translucent acrylic, are also attached with a couple of drops of nitrocellulose adhesive.

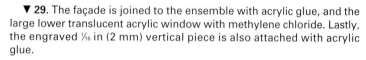
**▼ 29.** The façade is joined to the ensemble with acrylic glue, and the large lower translucent acrylic window with methylene chloride. Lastly, the engraved 1/16 in (2 mm) vertical piece is also attached with acrylic glue.

**◄ 30.** Before putting the large windows of the front façade into place, the inside of the ones that have already been attached is cleaned with a clean cloth soaked in alcohol, held with tweezers. This stops any dirt or stains from being left behind which would be impossible to remove later.

**►► 31.** The piece that will make up the large windows of the front façade is cut out and the front and sides are painted with metallic spray. The windows are glued in with methylene chloride. Note that the top window is left out, as the top floor has an open terrace.

▲ **32.** The top part is painted with metallic spray paint, after first protecting the rest with drafting tape. Once the paint is dry, the masks are removed. The paint on the part to be glued to the model should also be scraped off with a scalpel.

▲ **33.** The window piece is glued to the front façade, using acrylic glue in the center (the horizontal parts under the windows and the verticals) and methylene chloride in the upper part where it joins onto the roof pergola and the pillars on the terrace.

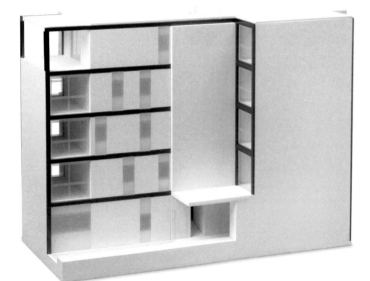

◄ **34.** Now the piece that separates the floors from the rear façade is glued on with methylene chloride.

► **35.** The front and side blinds are painted with metallic spray paint and the center with speckled synthetic paint in gray tones, after first masking out the areas not to be sprayed.

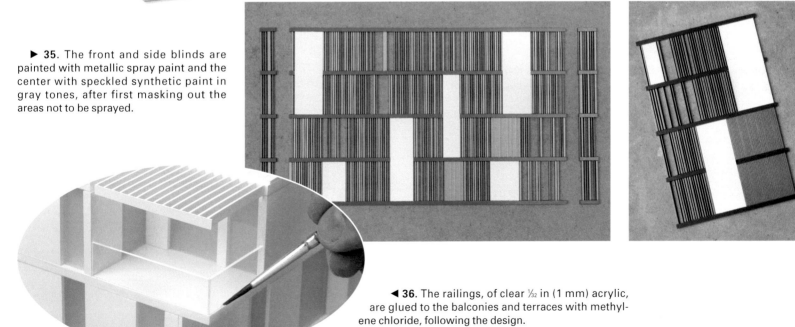

◄ **36.** The railings, of clear ½₂ in (1 mm) acrylic, are glued to the balconies and terraces with methylene chloride, following the design.

▲ **37.** The blinds are put into place, starting at one end of the front façade. First, the paint is removed with a scalpel from the areas where the blinds are to be joined to the façade, then the blinds are attached with methylene chloride. The blinds piece is then fixed at the other end.

▲ **38.** The front blinds are also glued with methylene chloride, which is applied with a fine brush to the places where the piece will join with the underlying façade. Next, the support strips are removed by twisting them gently with pliers.

◄ **39.** The rear part of the front blinds is touched up; the top crossbeam, for instance, is painted with metallic paint, applied with a fine soft-haired brush.

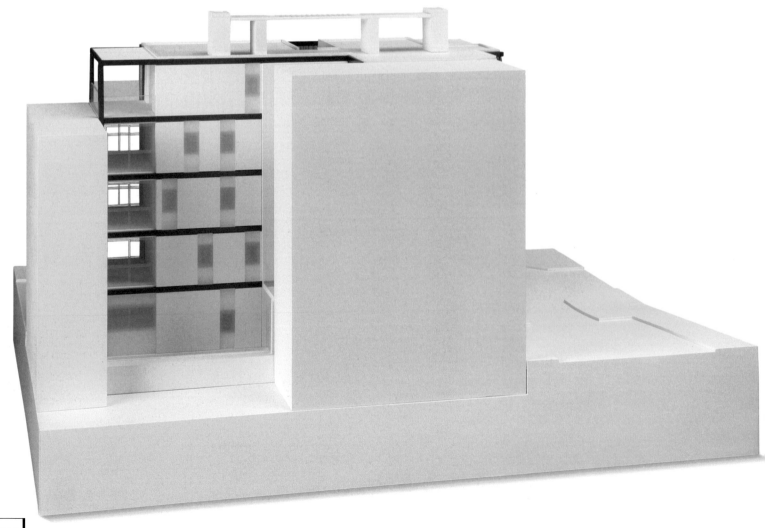

◀ **40.** The parts for the roof are attached, again using methylene chloride. To make this step easier, the paint has been removed with a scalpel from the areas of the join to ensure that they adhere properly, as no masking was carried out during painting.

▼ **41.** The sides of the base have been covered with a panel of white melamine (see page 68), and the top part has been given a coat of synthetic paint of the same color. This is done because filing the melamine could cause the paint to flake off. The model is now glued onto the base with acrylic glue.

◀▶ **42.** View of the finished model. Existing buildings have been represented as masses using white blocks, which are removable.

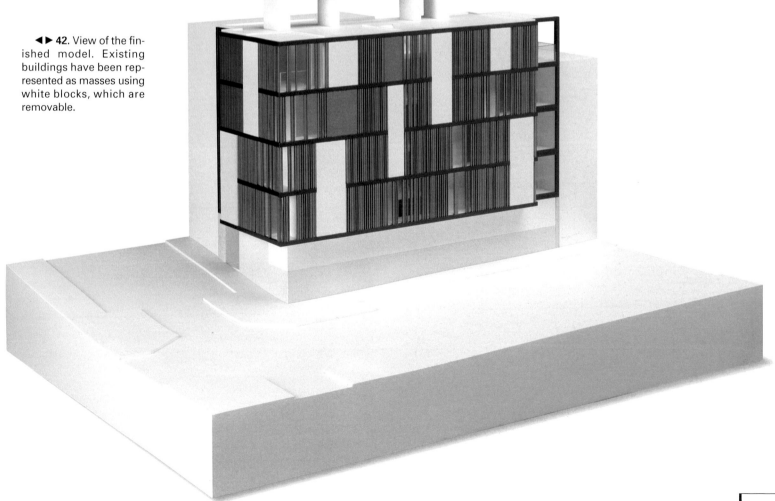

# High-speed train station

This step-by-step guide explains in great detail how the architectural model of a high-speed train station, 3 miles (5 km) from the city of Cuenca in Spain, was created, following the original design by GPO, S.A., an engineering and architectural company. The model, made by Pere and Ricard Pedrero, combines the representation of buildings along with the layout of the surroundings—such as access roads and car parks, which are shown partially—as well as the means of transport itself: the high-speed railway line. This presentation model shows in detail the façade and the main characteristics of the building, including the station, where the lines, trains, platforms, access points, and security systems are all indicated. The scale used is 1:160.

▼ **1.** Design plans in which the floor and the elevations can be seen. The first shows the interior layout of one of the wings of the building, which will be represented in the model because the building's roofs will be removable. The modelmaker's notes are also shown on the plans.

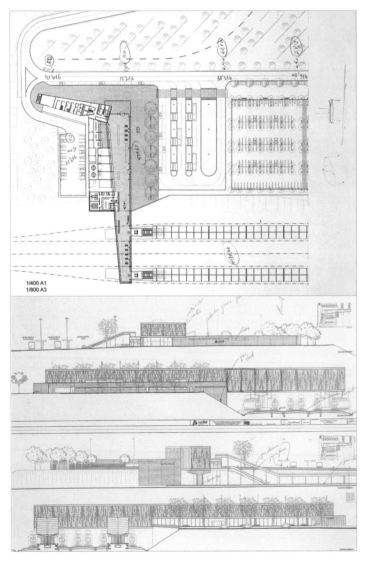

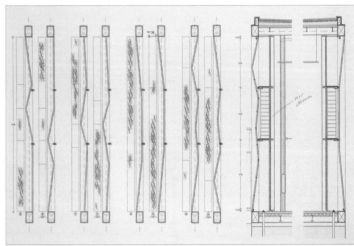

▲ **2.** Plan of the modules that make up the outer façade of the building's main wing, made up of undulating vertical slats arranged in a way that produces an interesting effect.

▼ **3.** Computer graphic view of the project in which the layout of the surroundings can also be observed.

▼ **4.** Assembly starts by producing the modules that make up the outer façade of the building's main wing. Taking the detailed plan as a reference, a two-module template is made; for this, the metal pieces are measured and glued onto a piece of wood covered with melamine, following the required layout. This will be used as a work surface.

▼▼ **5.** The horizontal crossbeams and vertical slats are laser-cut of ⅛ in (3 mm) acrylic (see the previous picture). The crossbeams are placed on the template, and tweezers are used to put the vertical slats into place one by one, following the plan. They are attached with methylene chloride.

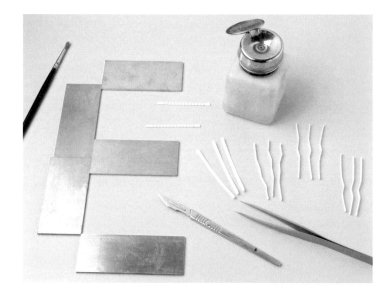

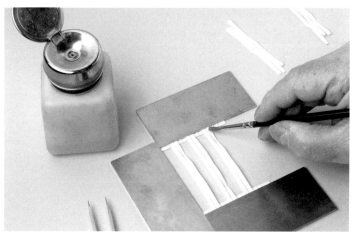

◀ **6.** The double template allows us to work on two modules at once, and by doing so, make rapid progress with the work.

▶ **7.** Next, the parts that will make up the structure of the façade are made of ¹⁄₃₂ in (1 mm) acrylic for the walls and long strips, and ¹⁄₁₆ in (2 mm) for the short strips.

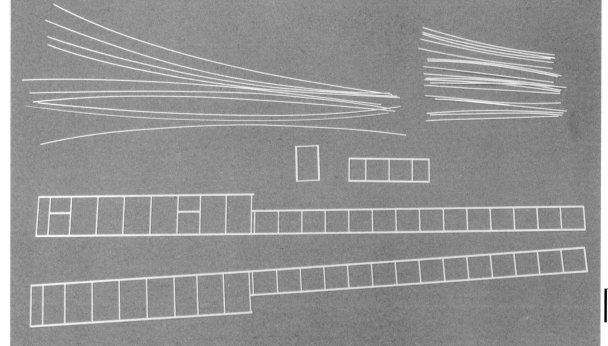

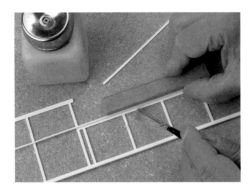

▲ **8.** Assembly starts by attaching the long strips in the form of crossbeams on the inside of the structure with methylene chloride, of which a small amount is applied to the joins. A block of MDF is used to stop the piece from moving and to prevent any unevenness during gluing.

▲ **9.** The ¹⁄₁₆ in (2 mm) strips that will be used as uprights for the modules are attached in the same way.

▲ **10.** The modules are attached with methylene chloride, using a fine soft hairbrush in the joins.

◀ **11.** The pieces that will make up the base and roof of this wing of the building are cut out. The first is made of engraved ¹⁄₁₆ in (2 mm) translucent acrylic (in the picture it still has its backing sheet) and the roof of opaque acrylic (here white), also ¹⁄₁₆ in (2 mm) thick.

▶ **12.** The join edges of the façade pieces are bevelled with the polishing machine. The façade is then assembled, taking the building's base piece as a guide.

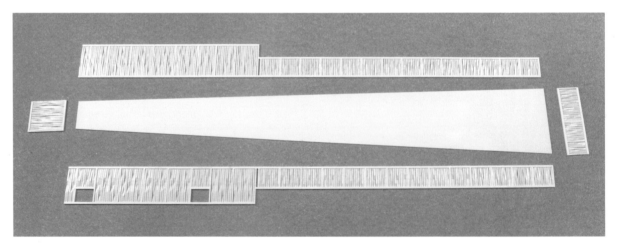

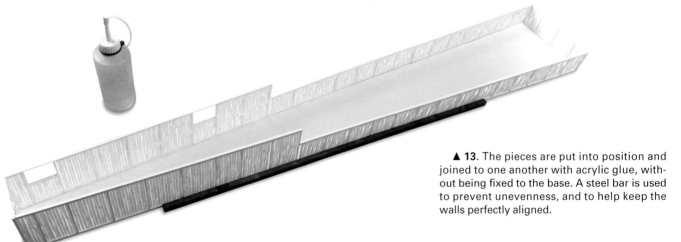

▲ **13.** The pieces are put into position and joined to one another with acrylic glue, without being fixed to the base. A steel bar is used to prevent unevenness, and to help keep the walls perfectly aligned.

◀ **14.** Once the adhesive is dry, the ensemble is covered with copper-colored synthetic paint. To do this, it is placed on a wooden base with a batten to help prevent unevenness and is attached with double-sided tape. It is left to dry.

▶ **15.** The pieces that will make up the inner façade are also made, using clear ⅟₁₆ in (2 mm) acrylic, to which gray vinyl has previously been applied; the apertures of the pieces are cut out and engraved by laser. Next, any excess vinyl is lifted off with a scalpel, taking care not to mark the acrylic.

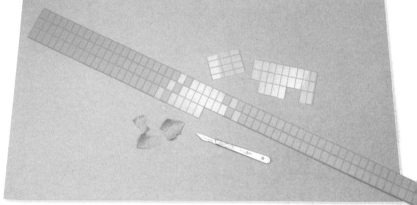

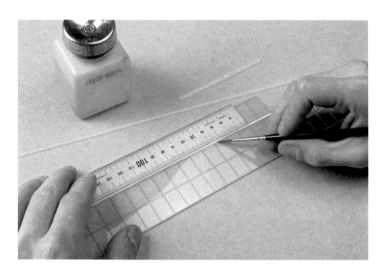

◀ **16.** Two ⅟₁₆ x ⅟₁₆ in (2 x 2 mm) strips of acrylic are fixed with methylene chloride onto the outside of each piece, on the face that is not covered with vinyl. The pieces are arranged horizontally, coinciding with the positions of the windows, and are attached using a ruler to ensure that they line up properly. This prevents any possible warping at the join with the outer façade.

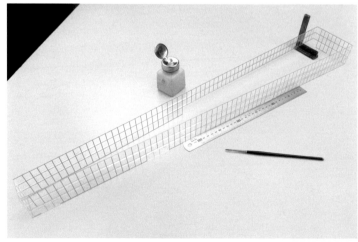

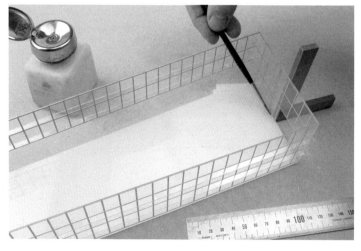

▲ **17.** The joins of the pieces are bevelled, and the model is assembled using methylene chloride. Care must be taken to position the end piece (at the back of the picture) against a set square to prevent any unevenness.

▲ **18.** Next, the ensemble is attached to the base with methylene chloride.

▼ **19.** The outer façade is also attached to the inner one, joining it by the strips with methylene chloride.

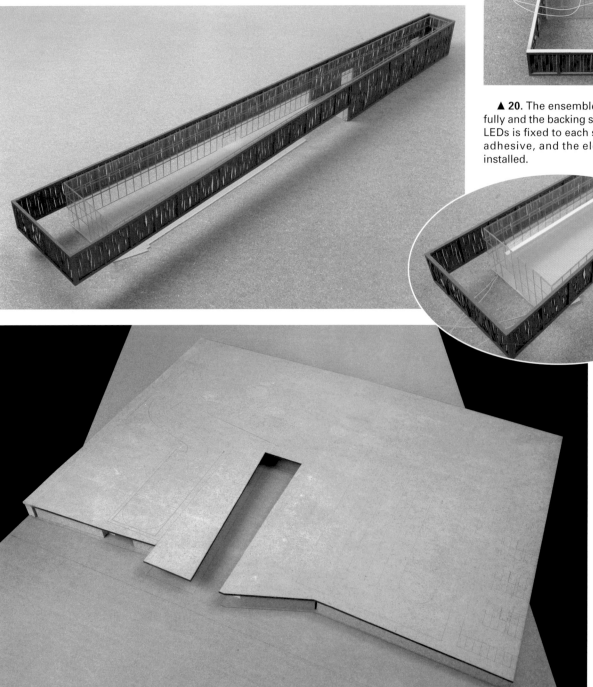

▲ **20.** The ensemble is turned around carefully and the backing sheet removed. A strip of LEDs is fixed to each side with cyanoacrylate adhesive, and the electric connections are installed.

▲ **21.** Following the design plans, a ³⁄₁₆ x ³⁄₁₆ in (4 x 4 mm) piece is cut out and attached to the center of the inside of one of the façades with methylene chloride.

◀ **22.** The base of the model, 2 x 56 x 48 in (5 x 142 x 122 cm), is made in MDF. The upper piece is added, with a height of 1½ in (3.5 cm) in one part and 1¾ in (4.5 cm) in another, following the incline shown in the plans. Here, the piece has been cut out and engraved by laser following the design.

▶ **23** The pieces that are to make up the pavements are cut out and engraved by laser in ¹⁄₃₂ in (1 mm) acrylic and are arranged on the base according to the layout given in the plans. Taking these as a guide, the position of the banks, platforms, and tracks is also marked.

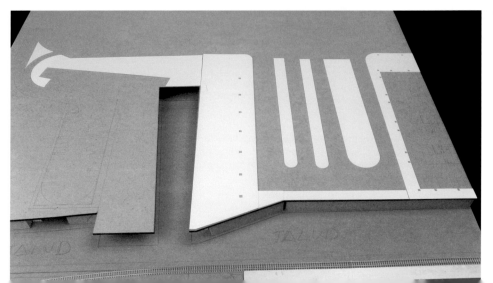

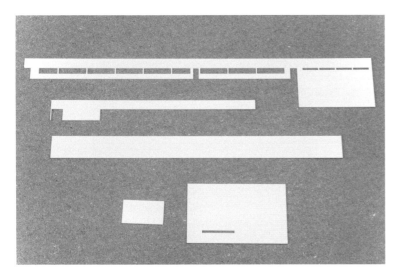

◄ **24.** Next, the walls of the building's secondary wing are made of ¹⁄₁₆ in (2 mm) acrylic, and the outer engraving is also done with the laser. They are painted with white synthetic paint.

► **25.** The pieces that make up the base are made the same way of ¹⁄₁₆ in (2 mm) acrylic, and joined with acrylic glue.

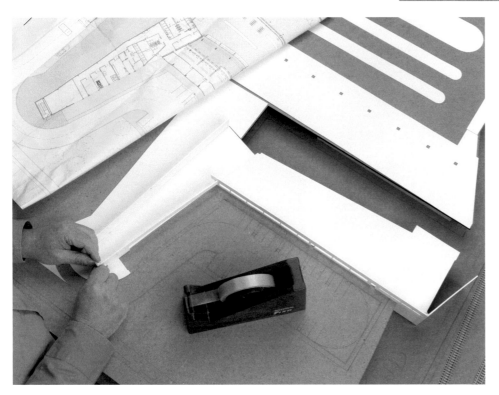

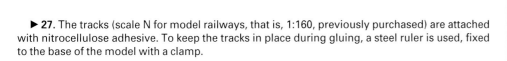

▲ **26.** Before assembly, it is essential to check that the work fits correctly into the model. Taking the plan at actual size as a reference, the piece that makes up the base is positioned on the model and the walls attached with adhesive tape.

► **27.** The tracks (scale N for model railways, that is, 1:160, previously purchased) are attached with nitrocellulose adhesive. To keep the tracks in place during gluing, a steel ruler is used, fixed to the base of the model with a clamp.

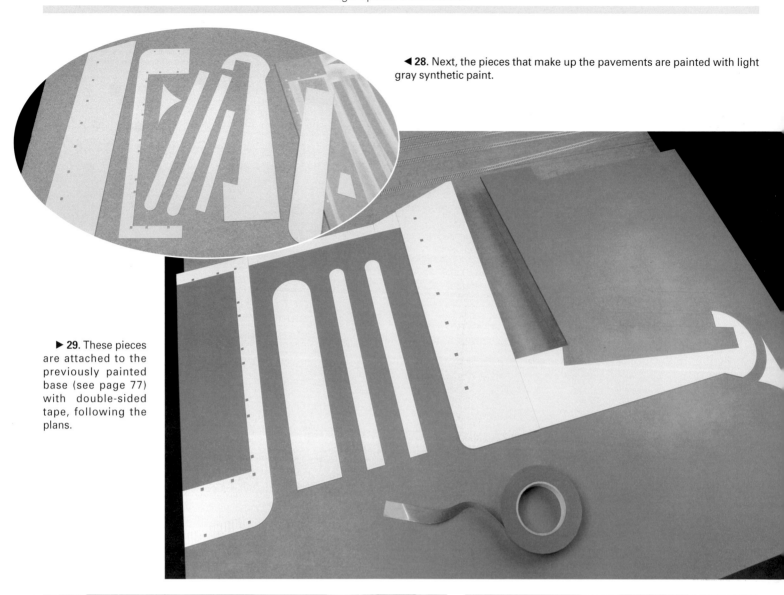

◄ **28.** Next, the pieces that make up the pavements are painted with light gray synthetic paint.

► **29.** These pieces are attached to the previously painted base (see page 77) with double-sided tape, following the plans.

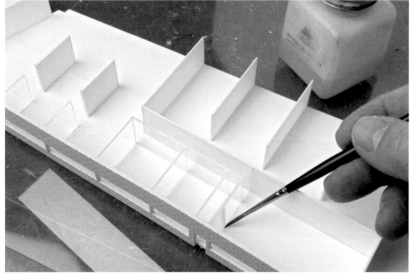

▲ **30.** The assembly of the building now begins. First, outer walls are attached, then the interior layout is assembled according to the plans. The dividers are made of both clear and white ⅟₃₂ in (1 mm) acrylic, and are attached with methylene chloride.

► **31.** The small walls or dividers and details are put in place with the help of the tweezers, and glued on with a drop of methylene chloride.

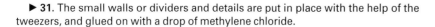

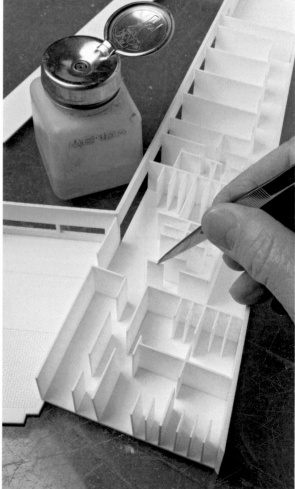

▲ **32.** The windows that will cover the apertures are made, of ⅟₃₂ in (1 mm) acrylic. This is clear acrylic, the reverse of which has been covered with translucent vinyl (see page 135), engraved and cut out by laser, then painted to simulate metal elements (see page 85).

▲ **33.** The window pieces are carefully fitted into the apertures, as they will also be visible from the inside; to do this, they are fitted by sanding the edges a little wherever necessary. They are then attached with a drop of methylene chloride in the corners.

► **34.** The pieces that represent the doors of the building (in dark gray) are made and fixed into place, following the processes described. This general view shows the piece once finished.

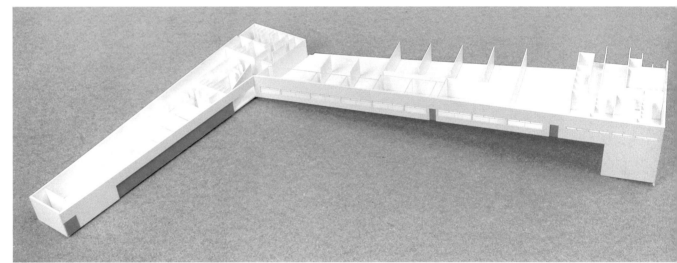

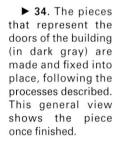

◄ ▼ **35.** Now, the pieces that will make up the roofs are cut out and engraved in ⅟₁₆ in (2 mm) acrylic. The pieces that make up the skylights are attached with methylene chloride and are painted gray using an airbrush.

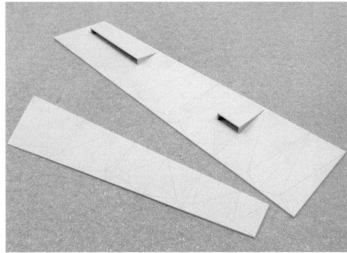

◄ **36.** Next, the banks that adjoin the track area must be made. The bank under the buildings is made of polyurethane foam (see pages 74–75), and the one that borders the model, on the other side of the tracks, is made using a sheet of MDF, bevel-cut at the top; this is fixed against the end of the base with PVA glue and several tacks, and is secured with a batten, also glued and nailed into place.

► **37.** The bank is made using a sheet of MDF with bevelled sides, which is also attached with PVA glue and several tacks.

◄ **38.** Two coats of PVA glue are applied to the polyurethane foam to make it more resistant and rigid. The glue is left to dry between each application.

► **39.** Gray melamine is used to veneer the sides of the model (see page 68). The building is positioned in the correct location within the model and the remaining pavements are attached with double-sided tape.

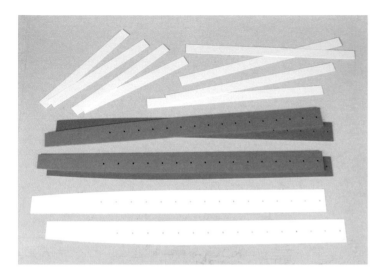

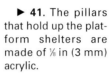

◄ **40.** It is now time to work on the pieces that will make up the platforms: ³⁄₁₆ in (4 mm) gray acrylic is used for the base (no 8 mm acrylic was available, as required by the design, so two pieces were made of ³⁄₁₆ in (4 mm) acrylic and then combined); the top of the platforms is made of ¹⁄₁₆ in (2 mm) acrylic and then engraved (at bottom of picture); the roofs of the shelters (top) are made of ¹⁄₁₆ in (1 mm) acrylic, also engraved.

► **41.** The pillars that hold up the platform shelters are made of ⅛ in (3 mm) acrylic.

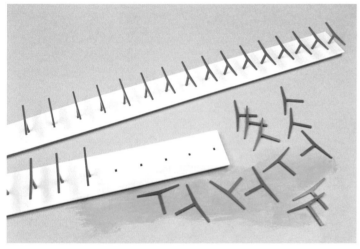

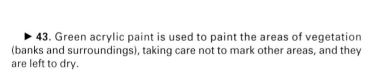

▲ **42.** The fit of all the pieces is checked before painting.

► **43.** Green acrylic paint is used to paint the areas of vegetation (banks and surroundings), taking care not to mark other areas, and they are left to dry.

◄ **44.** The pieces that make up the base of the platforms are joined with methylene chloride and attached to the model with acrylic glue.

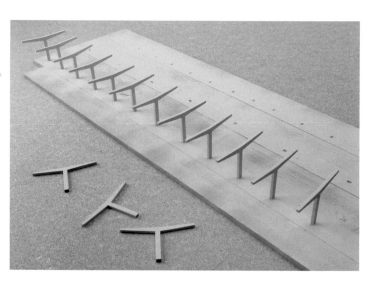

**◄ ► 45.** The platform pieces and the pillars are painted with gray synthetic paint, using an airbrush.

**◄ 46.** To ensure that the pieces fit correctly, they are arranged following the layout that they will later adopt alongside the buildings.

**► 47.** Next, the track ballast (the layer of crushed stone that is spread across the ground to provide a base for the ties of the tracks) is put onto the model. To prevent the gravel from falling off, a leftover piece of acrylic is attached to each end with drafting tape, which also serves to protect the platforms.

**◄ 48.** The gravel is applied (see page 90) and fixed into place by sprinkling the ensemble with a solution of PVA glue in water, using an airbrush. Several applications must be made, leaving them to dry each time, until the track ballast has adhered well. The pieces of acrylic can then be removed from the sides and the masking of the platforms.

**◄ 49.** The pillars that are to hold up the main wing of the building suspended over the tracks are made.

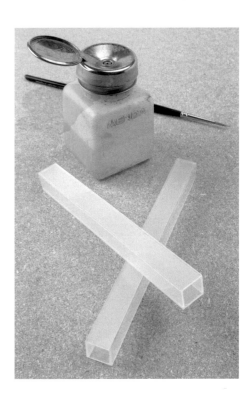

**► 50.** Next, the pillars are set in the correct position under the building to ensure that they fit within the model (here, the shaft of the pillar had to be cut to the right dimensions). After removing the layer of paint, the shaft is attached to the top of the column with methylene chloride. It is then painted with synthetic gray paint.

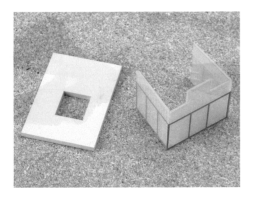

**▲ 51.** The pieces that will make up the elevators are also made. The base, which is shown with the elevator shaft, is made of ³⁄₁₆ in (4 mm) acrylic. The gallery (reached by elevator) is made of clear ¹⁄₃₂ in (1 mm) acrylic, with translucent vinyl on the interior, and the frames of the windows are made following the system used in the building's main wing (see step 17).

**▲ 52.** The pieces are glued with methylene chloride, using a fine brush in the inner joins.

**► 53.** Likewise, the elevator cabins are made of clear ¹⁄₁₆ in (2 mm) acrylic covered with translucent vinyl.

▲ **54.** The cabin pieces are cut to the required measurement and attached with methylene chloride.

▼ **55.** The stairs are made of ½₂ in (1 mm) acrylic.

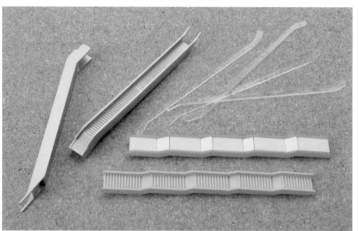

▼ **56.** The handrails of the escalator are also made of ½₂ in (1 mm) acrylic, this time clear, and attached with methylene chloride.

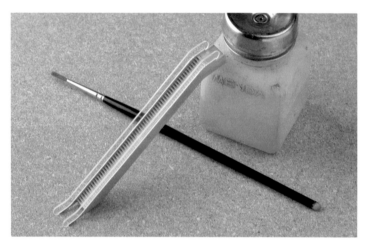

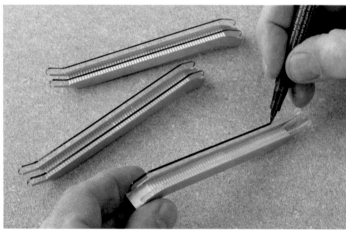

▲ **57.** The edge of the railings is painted with black permanent marker to represent the rubber handrail.

▶ **58.** The modelmaker makes a last-minute change, altering the slope and the dimensions of the model's outer bank. To do this, part of the track ballast is removed and a new piece of medium-density fiber-board is attached, following the process already described. A coat of green acrylic paint is applied.

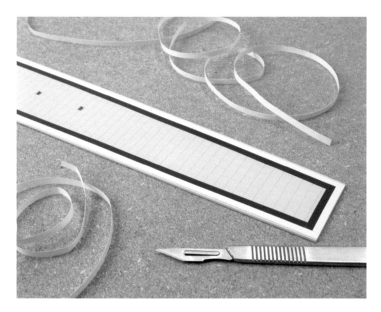

◄ **59.** Strips of red and white self-adhesive vinyl are attached to the platform pieces to represent the platform markings. The platforms are also attached to their bases with double-sided tape.

▲ ▼ **60.** The roofs of the platform shelters and the lampposts are spray-painted with silver bodywork paint. In this case, lampposts sold at a scale of 1:200 are used.

► **61.** The shelters of the station car park are made of ½₂ in (1 mm) acrylic. The sides and roof are painted in a similar way to the roofs of the platforms, as is the rear of the clear acrylic.

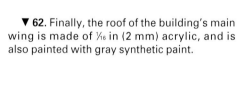

▼ **62.** Finally, the roof of the building's main wing is made of ¹⁄₁₆ in (2 mm) acrylic, and is also painted with gray synthetic paint.

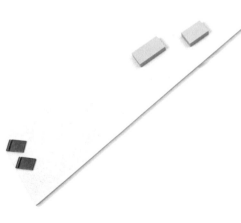

► **63.** Assembly starts by first attaching the secondary wing of the building, that is, the white piece, to the base of the model with acrylic glue. The main wing is then slotted into place with the other part of the building. Elements of the interior layout of the main wing can be seen in the picture, as well as one of the entrance doors which were made before assembly begins.

▲ **64.** The green areas are made (see page 91) and general assembly begins by attaching the pillars under the main building, the elevators, and the stairs.

◀ **65.** The pillars of the platforms and the roofs are also assembled. The circular columns that hold up the roofs over the stairs are added. These are made out of ¹⁄₁₆ in (2 mm) diameter polystyrene strips.

► **66**. To finish off, the shelters are placed within the parking area, the lampposts are put into place, and the parking spaces are marked out with fine polystyrene thread. General background elements like trees and vehicles are added.

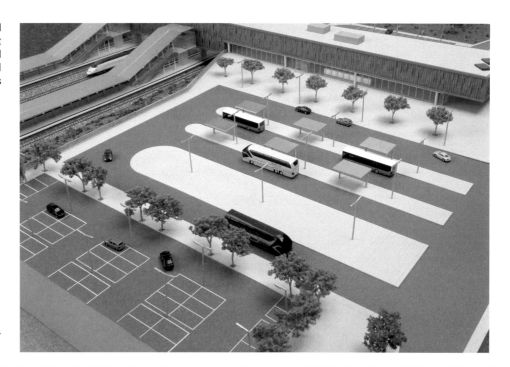

▼ **67**. The electrical installation is completed and the model is finished.

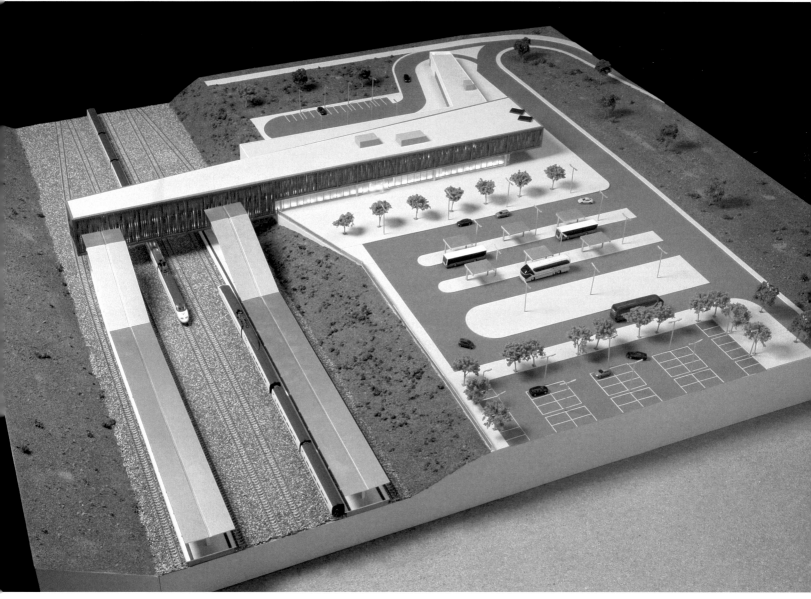

# Stand for a trade fair

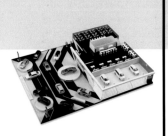

This is the architectural model of a stand for the automobile company SEAT at the 2009 Geneva Motor Show, following the original design of the design studio Picó & Asociados, made by Ricard Pedrero. The step-by-step guide here shows the whole process involved in creating an architectural model. This is a presentation model that reflects the stand's general architectural design, representing in great detail the colors and finishes of the elements that make it up. The vehicle exhibition area is visible, including numerous items of exhibition furniture (display cases and stands), as well as signs and screens. The layout of the top floor of the construction is also shown, including items of furniture. The creation of this model is a complex process, because it involves creating both architectural elements and furniture.

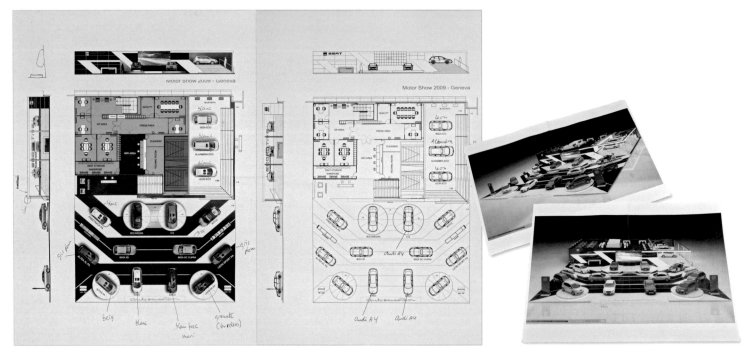

▲ **1.** An architectural model is made to a scale of 1:87 based on the original design of the stand by Picó & Asociados design studios. The original plans of the bottom floor of the stand, with its front and side elevations, can be seen in the picture. The modelmaker will use these as a guide during the entire process, making notes as needed to assist during the work.

▲ **2.** The computer graphic images created by the designers are also used as a guide. These show the layout of the top floor.

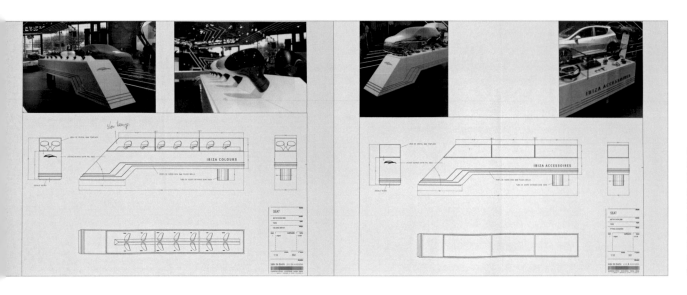

◄ **3.** The accessory display cases on the bottom floor, showing the range of car colors, are also made following the original design. The designers have drawn up specific plans for each element of the exhibition.

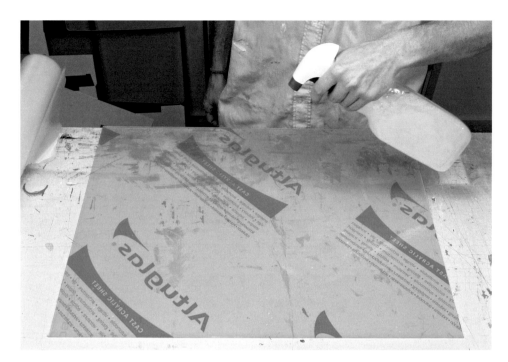

◄ **4.** The first step consists of making the stand's paved area. A 24 x 20 in (600 x 500 mm) sheet of clear glossy 1/16 in (2 mm) acrylic, cut in advance, is to be used for this. In the design, the paved area is based on a combination of black and white, meaning that the sheet will need painting. The design is faithfully reproduced by making vinyl paint masks on what will later be the underside of the paved area. The sheet is cleaned to remove any remnants of dust and dirt, and soapy water is applied with an atomiser.

► **5.** The vinyl is placed on the sheet of damp acrylic and pressed down with the hand.

▼ **6.** To ensure that the vinyl will adhere, excess water and any bubbles must be removed by pressing down firmly with a scraper from the center to the edges of the piece.

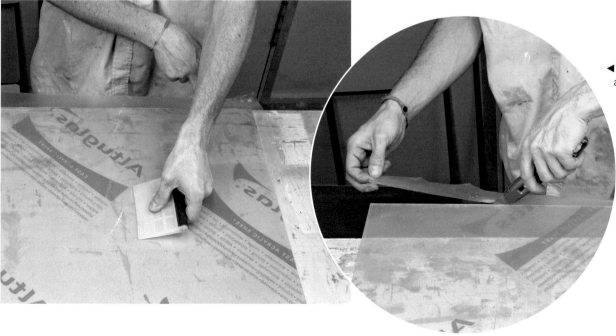

◄ **7.** Excess vinyl is cut away with a utility knife and the operation is repeated on the other side of the sheet; white vinyl has been used, as in this case the manufacturer's backing sheet was in poor condition. It is left to dry for 1 hour.

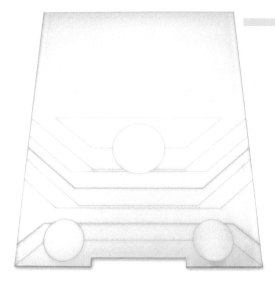

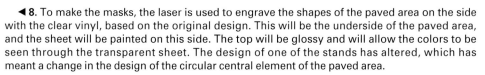

◀ **8.** To make the masks, the laser is used to engrave the shapes of the paved area on the side with the clear vinyl, based on the original design. This will be the underside of the paved area, and the sheet will be painted on this side. The top will be glossy and will allow the colors to be seen through the transparent sheet. The design of one of the stands has altered, which has meant a change in the design of the circular central element of the paved area.

◀ **9.** Taking the original design as a reference, with the help of a scalpel the masks are lifted from the spaces that are to be painted white, taking care not to mark the acrylic. They are cleaned with a cloth moistened with methylated spirit to remove any traces of paint and particles.

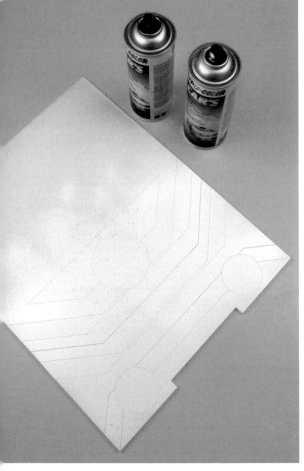

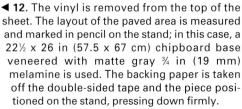

▲ **10.** Special matte white car spray paint is applied to the area and left to dry; a second layer is then applied. Once dry, the remaining masks are peeled off, and the vinyl covering the inner face of the sheet is removed. Two coats of black paint are applied following the same process.

▲ **11.** Once the paint is dry, the paved area is attached to the stand with wide double-sided tape. Glue is not used because this could damage the layer of paint. The tape is positioned lengthwise on the painted side without removing the backing paper, and a scraper is then used to remove any bubbles and irregularities. Any excess is cut away with a utility knife.

◀ **12.** The vinyl is removed from the top of the sheet. The layout of the paved area is measured and marked in pencil on the stand; in this case, a 22½ x 26 in (57.5 x 67 cm) chipboard base veneered with matte gray ¾ in (19 mm) melamine is used. The backing paper is taken off the double-sided tape and the piece positioned on the stand, pressing down firmly.

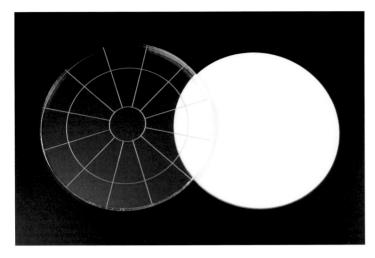

▲ **13.** The pieces that will make up the stands are laser-cut following the original plans. The top pieces are of clear ⅛ in (3 mm) acrylic, engraved according to the design. The bottom pieces are made of white ¹⁄₃₂ in (1 mm) acrylic; they are cut about ¹⁄₁₆ in (2 mm) too small so they appear to be hidden supports used to raise the stand.

▲ **14.** The undersides of the stands are painted white (the side that has been engraved). The top and sides of the piece are protected with drafting tape.

◀ **15.** The same paint as that used on the paved area is applied (special white matte car spray paint) and left to dry; a second layer is then applied. Once dry, the drafting tape is removed.

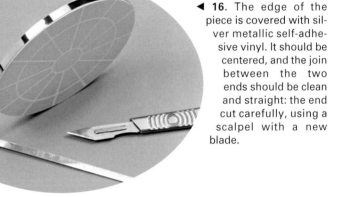

◀ **16.** The edge of the piece is covered with silver metallic self-adhesive vinyl. It should be centered, and the join between the two ends should be clean and straight: the end cut carefully, using a scalpel with a new blade.

▲ **17.** The top piece of the stand is joined on its painted side to the bottom piece with double-sided tape, ensuring that it is properly centered.

▶ **18.** The piece that makes up the stand's paved area is cleaned with methylated spirit to remove dirt and any traces of grease caused by handling. Next, the stands are attached with double-sided tape, centered on the circular elements of the paved area. They are positioned so that the join of the silver edging is at the back.

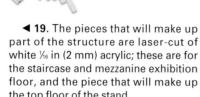
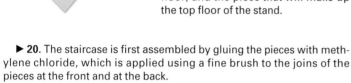
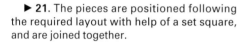
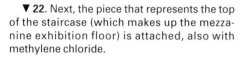

◀ **19.** The pieces that will make up part of the structure are laser-cut of white ¹⁄₁₆ in (2 mm) acrylic; these are for the staircase and mezzanine exhibition floor, and the piece that will make up the top floor of the stand.

▶ **20.** The staircase is first assembled by gluing the pieces with methylene chloride, which is applied using a fine brush to the joins of the pieces at the front and at the back.

▶ **21.** The pieces are positioned following the required layout with help of a set square, and are joined together.

▼ **22.** Next, the piece that represents the top of the staircase (which makes up the mezzanine exhibition floor) is attached, also with methylene chloride.

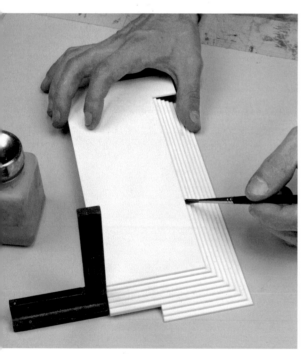

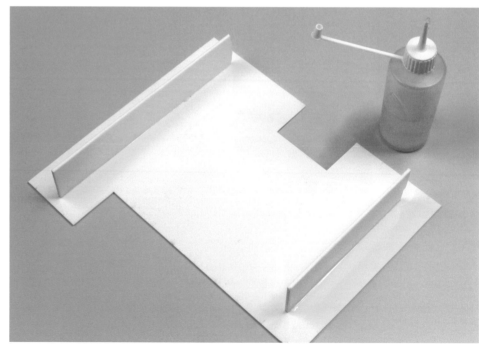

▶ **23.** Two supports are attached with acrylic glue to the underside of the piece that makes up the top floor of the stand. These supports are made using leftover pieces of ¹⁄₁₆ in (2 mm) acrylic; they will be somewhat shorter than the floor piece.

◄ **24.** The top floor is joined to the mezzanine exhibition floor. To do this, a piece of 1/16 in (2 mm) acrylic is cut out to a width that is sufficient for the side edge of the top floor to coincide perfectly with the side edge of the mezzanine floor. The piece will be smaller than the join and will be glued on with methylene chloride, with the help of a set square to ensure that it is aligned properly.

▲ **25.** The pieces of smoked black 1/64 in (0.5 mm) acrylic that will make up the side walls of the stand are cut out and engraved by laser.

▲ **26.** The underside of each piece (the unengraved side) is cleaned with methylated spirit and a cloth.

▲ **27.** Following the process described for the paved area, matte vinyl is attached to the underside of the pieces, using soapy water.

▲ **28.** Any bubbles and excess water are removed by pressing down firmly with a scraper from the center to the edges. The pieces are left to dry for 1 hour, the excess vinyl is cut away with a scalpel, and the edges are polished with sandpaper.

▶ **29.** The walls are put into the structure to ensure that they fit well, holding them in place temporarily with drafting tape. A further wall is added to check that the structure of the top floor lines up with the mezzanine exhibition floor, and is then removed. The matte vinyl covering makes the walls more opaque, preventing the underside of the stand from being seen.

▼ **30.** The walls are dismantled and the top floor is painted black. The mezzanine floor and the stairs are protected with newspaper. This is held in place with drafting tape and a layer of special matte black car spray paint is applied. It is left to dry and another coat is applied.

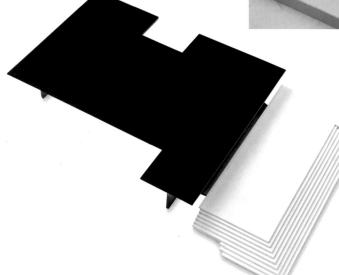

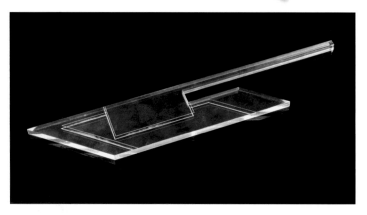

▲ **31.** The walls of the stand are now permanently assembled. Note that the back wall has been cut to adapt it to the shape of the floor. The vertical edges of the pieces (those that are to be joined) are first bevelled with the polishing machine, except for those right at the front, and they are filed to get a perfect finish. They are held together with drafting tape and glued with methylene chloride. Finally, several supports are added to the underside of the construction (see step 23).

▲ **32.** A piece of clear 2 in (5 cm) acrylic that will form part of the front of the stand is cut out and engraved by laser following the plans. A bar of acrylic with the same thickness and dimensions as the piece is also cut.

▶ **33.** Primer is applied and the piece is painted with special car spray paint. Masks are made using drafting tape and the paint is applied to all sides of the piece. The bar, which was painted earlier, is glued on with methylene chloride.

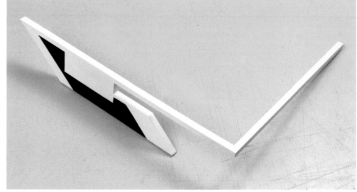

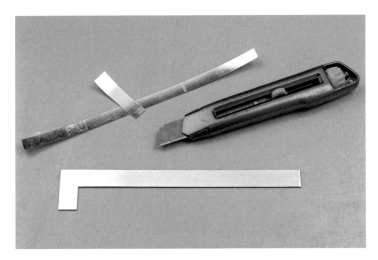

▲ **34**. The piece that will make up the back wall of the mezzanine exhibition floor is cut out of ⅟₃₂ in (1 mm) acrylic, and silver metallic vinyl is attached to the front surface.

▲ **35**. The silver piece is attached with methylene chloride to the side wall of the structure, as well as to the top floor and the mezzanine floor, making up its back wall. Next, the front piece is attached to the front wall of the stand and to the end of the right side with double-sided tape. This is done to prevent problems with the paint, as the acrylic glue could spoil the paint, the methylene chloride could run off it, and the pieces might not adhere. Finally, three walls are made on the inside of the stand's lower entrance to form a corner.

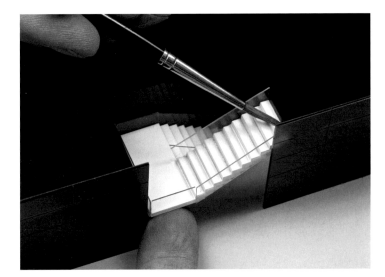

◀ **36**. The staircase is made of ⅟₁₆ in (2 mm) acrylic for the steps and the landing, and transparent green ⅟₆₄ in (0.5 mm) acrylic for the banisters; this is carefully attached to the structure with methylene chloride.

▲ **37**. Next, the video screen wall and the sign that is to appear on the mezzanine exhibition floor are printed on paper in different sizes, as there may be small variations in the model compared to the original plans. Once the measurements have been checked, they are cut out with a utility knife and glued onto pre-cut pieces of ⅟₁₆ in (2 mm) acrylic with double-sided tape.

◀ **38**. The video screen is attached to the front of the façade with double-sided tape and the sign on the mezzanine floor is glued on with methylene chloride. In order to position the sign at the correct height, two ⅛ in (3.2 mm) polystyrene bars are put in place as supports. Once it has adhered correctly, the supports are removed. The front staircase is also glued on with methylene chloride, for which a prefabricated 34° piece in polystyrene has been used, cut to the required measurement.

▲ **39.** The pieces that will make up the interior room on the top floor (designed for use as the kitchen) are laser-cut, as are the pieces that will make up the seats and stools on the top floor. The latter have been engraved to imitate the padded effect of the original seating.

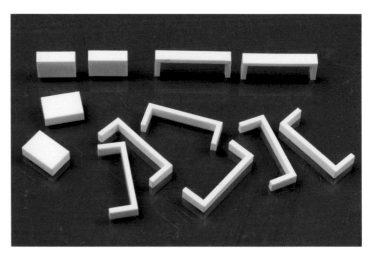

▲ **40.** Pieces of white ³⁄₁₆ in (5 mm) acrylic that will make up the bars and the bar counters are also cut out. More pieces than are necessary are cut out in case some of them are spoilt.

▲ **41.** In addition, the inner panels of the counters are cut out of black ¹⁄₃₂ in (1 mm) acrylic and engraved. Next, silver spray paint is applied with a brush; the paint is sprayed onto a fragment of leftover acrylic and applied to the engraved motif with the brush. It is left to dry and any excess is removed with a clean cloth dampened with alcohol.

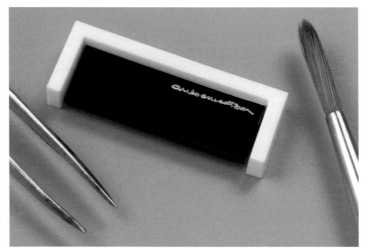

◀ **42.** The panels are attached to the central bottom part of the counters with methylene chloride, holding them in place with the tweezers.

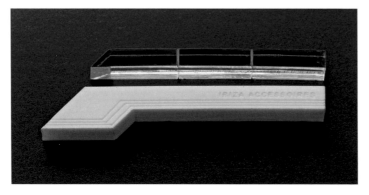

▲ **43.** The exhibition display cases that are to be located at the bottom of the stand are made, using white ¼ in (6 mm) acrylic for the bottom, and transparent acrylic of the same thickness for the top. In both cases, the pieces with motifs are cut out and engraved by laser according to the design.

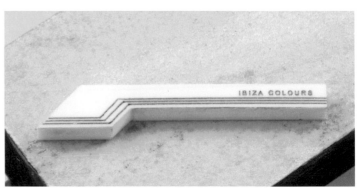

▲ **44.** Silver paint is applied to the engraved motifs with a brush, following the process already described. It is left to dry and the excess is removed by rubbing the piece on a sandpaper block.

◀ **45.** The piece of clear acrylic that makes up the top of the display cases is given a translucent effect by rubbing it with sandpaper, and then glued on with methylene chloride. Finally, a polystyrene tube painted with silver spray paint is positioned at the end of the display case to form a foot.

◀ **46.** The panels that are to be placed at the entrance to the stand are also made in smoked black ¹⁄₃₂ in (1 mm) acrylic, with the cutting and engraving done by laser. Once the panel has been cut out, the self-adhesive transfer of the brand and logo is applied. The base is made by gluing together two pieces of gray ¹⁄₃₂ in (1 mm) acrylic with methylene chloride. The transfer of the logo and brand is also applied to the front wall of the stand, as well as to the back wall of the mezzanine floor and on the outside.

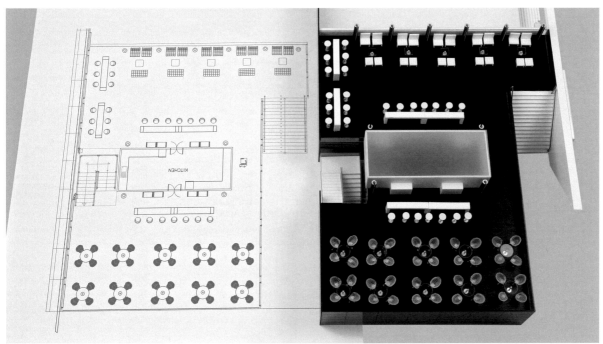

◀ **47.** The walls and the roof (made of translucent acrylic) that make up the kitchen on the top floor of the stand are glued on, and this ensemble is attached following the layout of the plan. The furniture, made earlier, is then put into place (see page 81 and following).

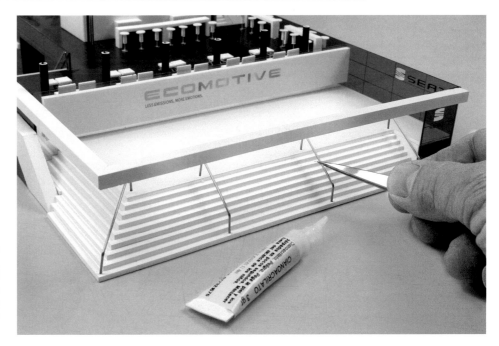

▶ **48.** The handrails for the stairs are made of ¹⁄₆₄ in (0.5 mm) diameter stainless-steel tube, which is bent with the help of pliers, and glued on with cyanoacrylate adhesive. Four are placed on the outer stairs and one on each side of the front staircase that leads to the top floor.

▲ **49.** Once the furniture has been put into the right position, it is fixed onto the structure. Nitrocellulose adhesive is used to join pieces that have a larger base or contact area with the floor, whilst cyanoacrylate adhesive is used for small pieces with a small base; accelerator is applied when necessary.

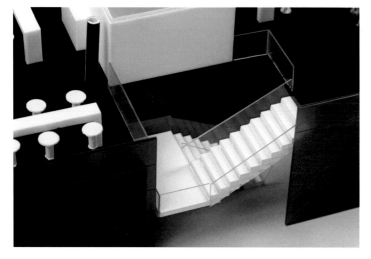

◀ **50.** The lamps have been made of ³⁄₁₆ in (4 mm) diameter polystyrene tube, painted with black spray paint, in which, once the paint is dry, a vertical incision has been made. Several square lamps have also been made in a similar way to the circular ones (see page 83).

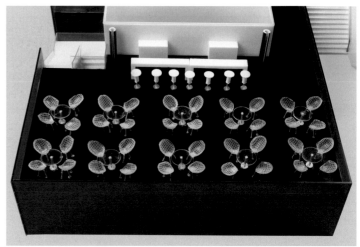

▲ **51.** The pieces of green ¹⁄₆₄ in (0.5 mm) acrylic that make up the handrail on the top floor are attached with methylene chloride.

▲ **52.** View of the layout of the furniture and the counters on the left-hand side of the top floor of the stand.

▲ ▼ **53.** The finished model.

# Property development

The following step-by-step guide shows the creation of an architectural model for a development of 190 homes, following the original design of Manolo Ortiz Alba (Oiskosvia arquitectura, s.c.c.l.) for Llinars Residencial, S.A. (Grup l'Ull Blau), produced by Pere Pedrero. This is a collection of different buildings which occupy almost the entire block where they are located. The presentation model aims to show the main features of the development to possible buyers, so it represents the general characteristics of the homes, façades and roofs as well as the planned layout of the surroundings, including both private and public spaces. In addition, it includes a general representation of the other buildings in the block, represented using massing elements, and the streets that surround it.

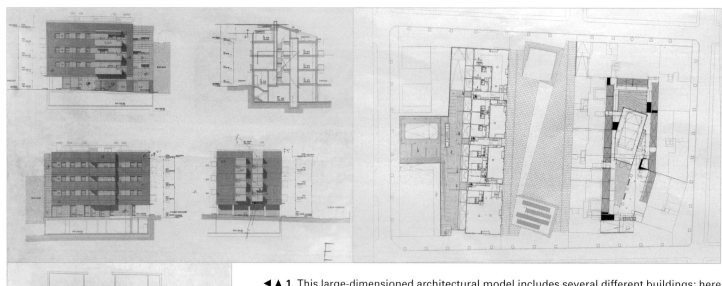

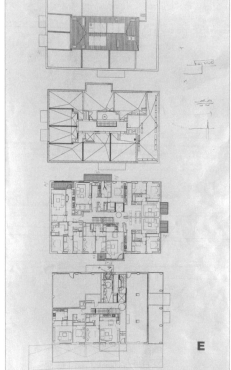

◄▲ **1.** This large-dimensioned architectural model includes several different buildings; here the step-by-step guide concentrates on making one of these buildings. The picture shows the elevations and different floors of the building (marked on the plan with the letter E), as well as the layout and distribution of the spaces that surround the buildings, with their key characteristics.

▼ **2.** The model is made at a scale of 1:100. After the pieces have been cut and engraved by laser in 1/16 in (2 mm) acrylic, the outer walls of the building are made. The joints are mitered, so the pieces are bevelled, and the joint edges trimmed to 45° with an electric polishing machine.

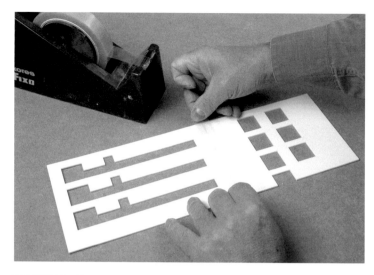

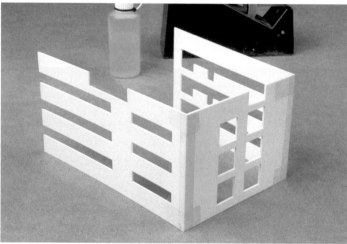

▲ **4.** The adhesive tape serves as a kind of hinge, keeping the joint in place while the adhesive dries. The same procedure is used on the other piece that makes up part of the building's façade. Once the adhesive is dry, the adhesive tape is removed.

▶ **5.** Next, the piece is spray-painted with light brown acrylic paint. To do this, it is placed on a base (a sheet of plywood) and attached with double-sided tape to stop it from moving.

◀ ▼ **3.** To make the joints, the walls are first fixed to the outside with adhesive tape. The work is turned upside down and acrylic glue is applied along the joint. Finally, the pieces are positioned at a right angle, depending on the required layout.

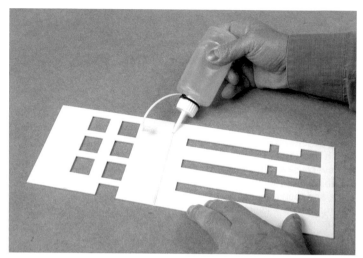

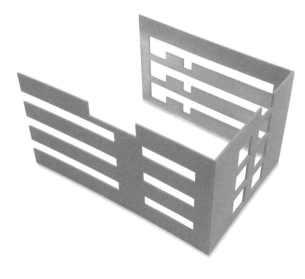

▲ **6.** The piece painted.

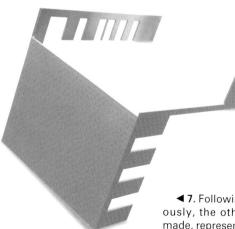

◀ **7.** Following the process described previously, the other part of the façade is also made, representing gray bricks.

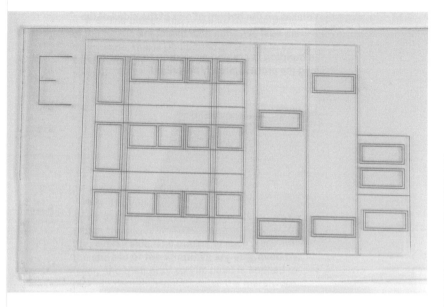

**▼ 21.** Having reached this point, the elements that will make up the façade of the gallery are made of ⅟₁₆ in (2 mm) acrylic, which is cut out and engraved by laser and then painted.

**▲ 23.** The join edges are bevelled with an electric sander and are attached with acrylic glue.

**◄ 19.** The building's outer gallery is now made. The window piece is produced first (at left), following the process described in step 9 and onwards.

**▼ 20.** The piece is cut out, the edges are bevelled with the polishing machine, and the work is assembled as shown in the picture; the joins are glued with a drop of methylene chloride.

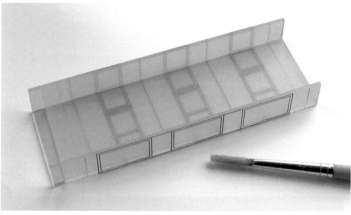

**▼ 22.** The pieces are cut out with the saw, following the plans. They are numbered and marked on the back so that they fit together perfectly once assembled.

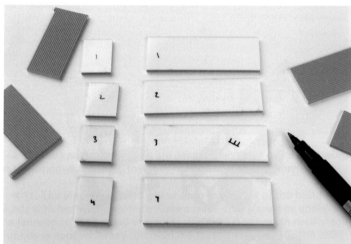

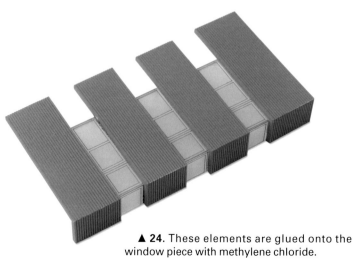

**▲ 24.** These elements are glued onto the window piece with methylene chloride.

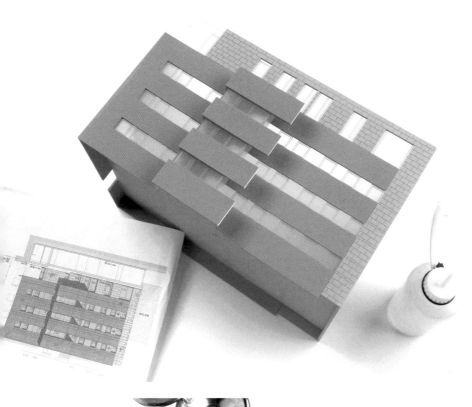

◀ **25.** Finally, the piece is attached to one of the building's façades with acrylic glue. Note how it matches the design, shown alongside.

▼ **26.** The balconies are made next. The pieces that make up the floor are first made of ⅟₁₆ in (2 mm) acrylic, and are painted in acrylic of the color stipulated in the design.

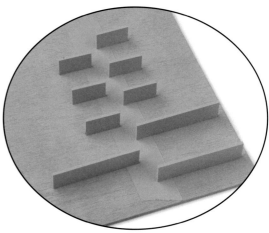

◀ **27.** The railing pieces are also cut out of clear ⅟₁₆ in (1.5 mm) acrylic with translucent vinyl on the underside, and are glued onto the base or floor of the balcony with methylene chloride. The railing pieces will be somewhat longer than is necessary; they too are glued with methylene chloride.

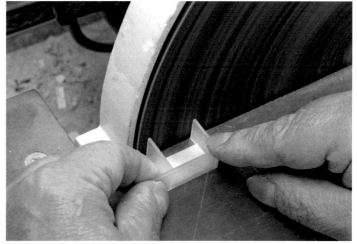

▲ **28.** Any excess material is removed with an electric polishing machine until the railings line up with the base or floor of the balcony. Other, excess material is removed from the front railing.

◀ **29.** The balconies are attached to the building's façade with methylene chloride. A small amount only is used on the join areas so that it does not drip and spoil the paint.

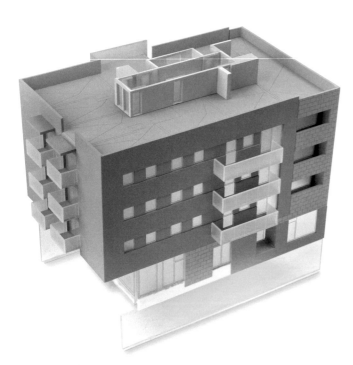

◄ **30.** Next, the attic piece is attached with acrylic glue. The pieces that are found between the windows and the eaves of the top balconies are also made. They are painted with gray acrylic paint and glued on with methylene chloride.

▲ **31.** The building's upper roof is made of ⅟₁₆ in (2 mm) tiled polystyrene sheet, and painted with acrylic paint.

▲ **32.** The pieces that represent the awnings of the balconies, pre-cut of clear ⅟₃₂ in (1 mm) acrylic, are then glued on with nitrocellulose adhesive.

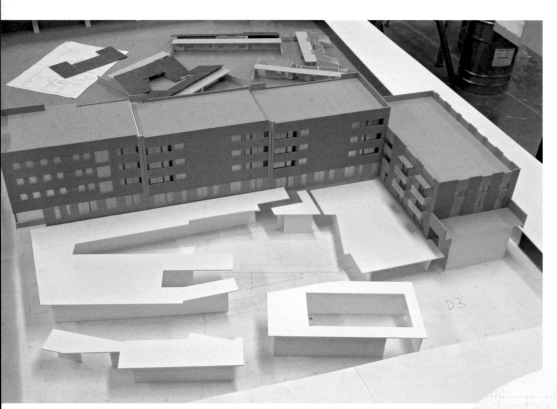

▲ **33.** Other buildings in the development are made following a process similar to that described. They are positioned on the base within the surroundings (the streets that surround the block) that have been made previously (see pages 76–77). To ensure that the buildings and pieces that make up the surroundings fit properly, an actual size plan of the model has been placed on the base as a template. The paving pieces of the building's private area are made of ⅟₁₆ in (2 mm) acrylic.

► **34.** The swimming pool (see pages 87 and following) that is to occupy the central part of the space is made. The wooden decking has been represented using bubinga wood veneer.

◄ **35.** The fit of building E is checked using the plan as a guide, and in relation to the pieces that make up the paving of the private space at the back. The swimming pool is also put in place to ensure a perfect fit.

▼ **36.** The work continues by creating other buildings in the development, located on the other side of the block. The paving pieces of the private area are also made of ¹⁄₁₆ in (2 mm) acrylic.

▼ **37.** The pieces that will make up the private terraces of the ground-floor apartments are produced.

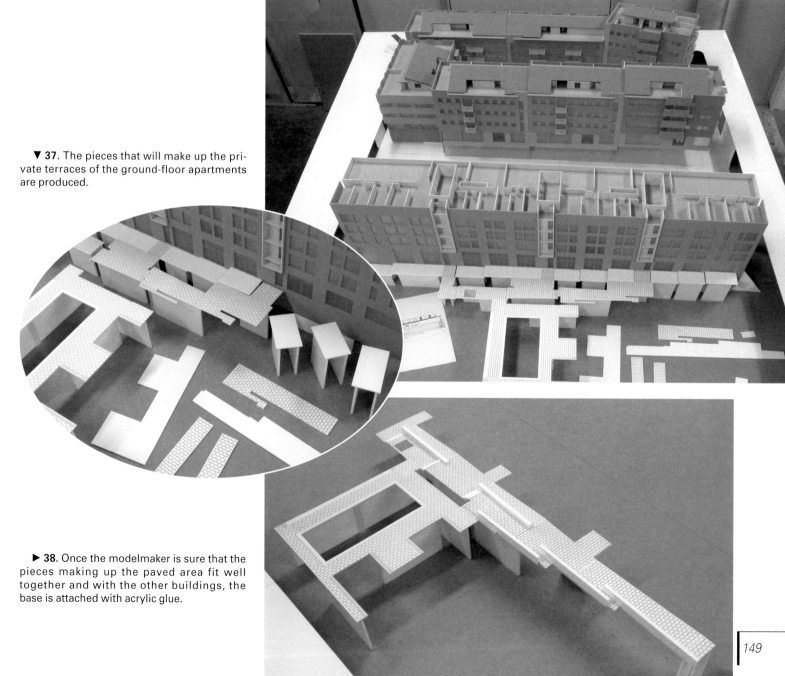

► **38.** Once the modelmaker is sure that the pieces making up the paved area fit well together and with the other buildings, the base is attached with acrylic glue.

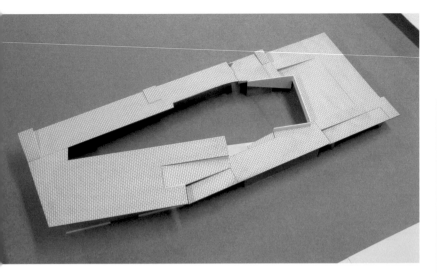

39. The same is done with the other paved area.

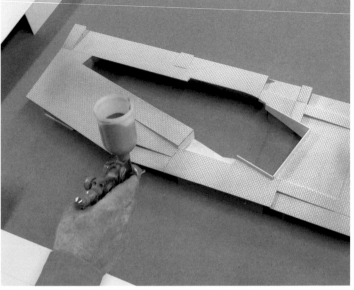

◄▲ 40. Next, the paved areas are painted. First, a thin coat of gray acrylic paint is applied with the airbrush to give a fine speckled effect, and left to dry. Then the paint is applied, making small strokes with a coarse-haired brush to represent the colors and texture of the paving. Excess paint is removed from the brush (in this case on a scrap of wood) before each application to avoid using too much paint and to achieve the desired irregular appearance.

▲ 41. A section of the painted paved area.

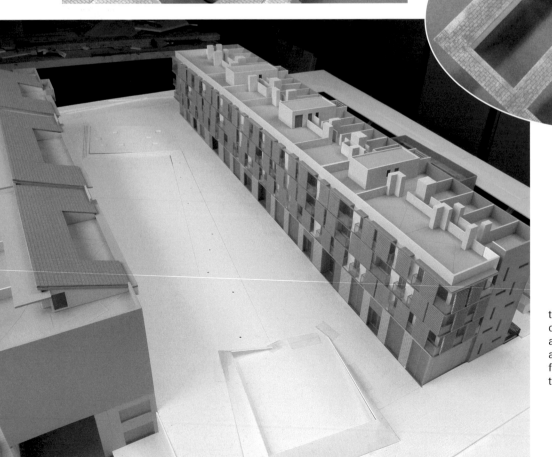

◄ 42. The pieces that will make up the central square of the block are made and introduced into the model. They are put in place according to the design, being provisionally attached with adhesive tape to check that they fit with the buildings that surround them and that are already in place.

▶ **43.** The pavements that surround the block are made; they are cut out and engraved by laser in ½₂ in (1 mm) acrylic, and then painted with clear gray acrylic paint using an airbrush.

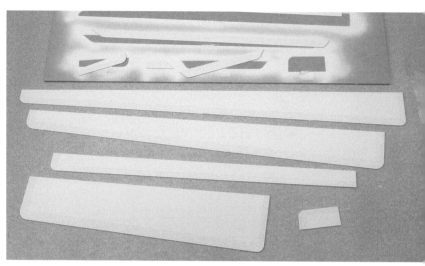

▼ **44.** The base is painted (see page 77) to represent the paving of the road, and the pieces that make up the pavement are attached with acrylic glue.

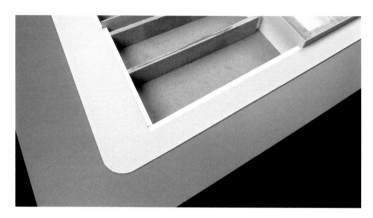

▶ **45.** The larger pieces that make up the central square of the block are attached with acrylic glue.

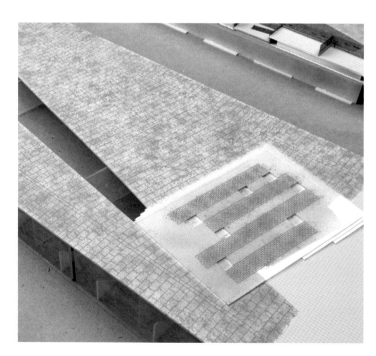

▲ **46.** One of the end pieces is put into place, and the central pieces are painted following the process described for the other paved areas.

▶ **47.** Next, the paved area of the end piece is painted in a uniform color.

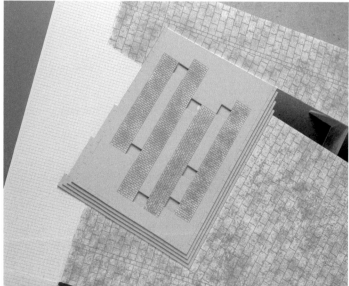

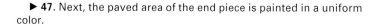

151

◀ **48.** The green area is made (see page 91) and is glued onto the model with acrylic glue. Narrow strips of ¹⁄₁₆ in (2 mm) acrylic have been attached to the inside of the aperture to support the piece.

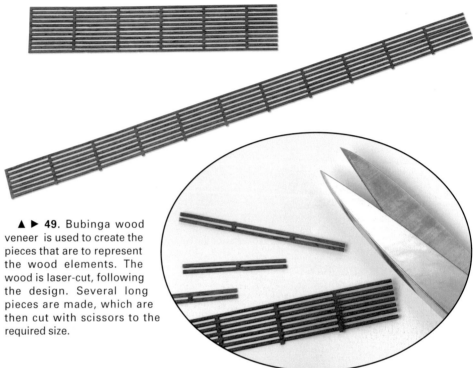

▲ ▶ **49.** Bubinga wood veneer is used to create the pieces that are to represent the wood elements. The wood is laser-cut, following the design. Several long pieces are made, which are then cut with scissors to the required size.

◀ **50.** Work continues, making the remaining green areas and putting the swimming pool into place. The outer fences are also made of ¹⁄₁₆ in (2 mm) painted acrylic, and are fixed to the base and to the paving pieces with acrylic glue. The fences for the terraces of the ground-floor apartments are also made, and the veneer is attached with nitrocellulose adhesive.

◀ **51.** The fences that divide the building's private roof terraces are made.

▼ **52.** View of part of the model with the completed wooden elements.

▼ **53.** The other buildings in the model are put into place. Those that are not part of the development are represented as masses and are painted light gray.

▲ 54. The pieces that will make up the chimneys of the buildings are made and painted.

◀ 55. Chimneys are attached to the roofs of all the buildings. The fences that surround the swimming pool are added. These are made of engraved, clear ¹⁄₃₂ in (1.5 mm) acrylic, and are attached with nitrocellulose adhesive.

▲ 56. The outer fences, made previously (see page 84), and the pillars, made of ¹⁄₁₆ x ¹⁄₁₆ in (2 x 2 mm) acrylic, are also attached.

◀ 57. The piece that will make up the children's play area is painted red and is attached following the system described for the green area. The paving slabs are also attached to the green area.

▶ 58. Nitrocellulose adhesive is used to attach the play equipment to the children's play area, as well as the remaining furniture in the square (see page 83). To set the trees on the model, the holes into which the trunks will be inserted must be made, using a rotary tool fitted with the correct bit.

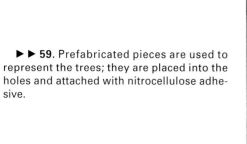

▶▶ 59. Prefabricated pieces are used to represent the trees; they are placed into the holes and attached with nitrocellulose adhesive.

► **60.** Finally, the streetlights and cars (pre-fabricated pieces) are arranged and glued into place.

▼ **61.** The finished model.

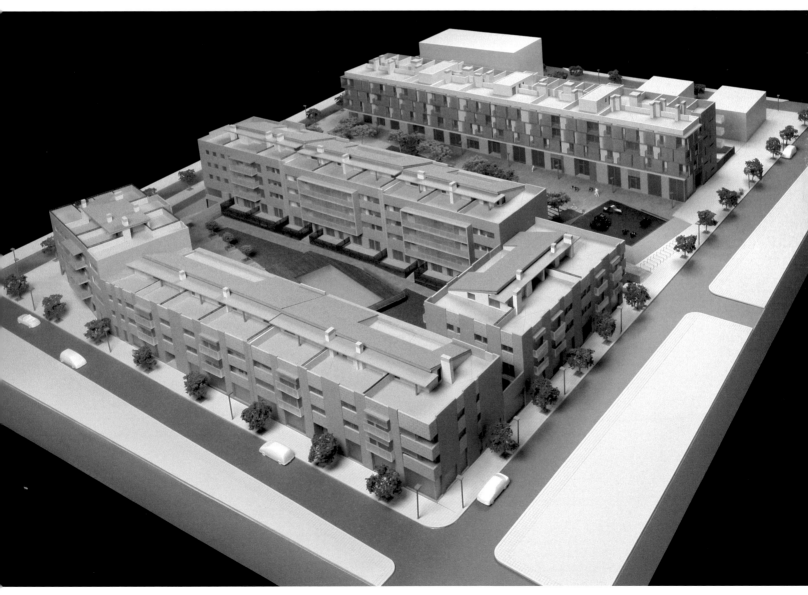

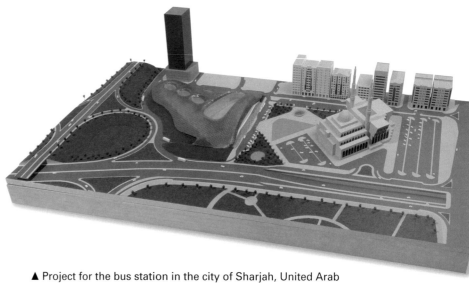

▲ Project for the bus station in the city of Sharjah, United Arab Emirates, Xavier Fabré and Mercè Torras, architects. Architectural model of acrylic and sheet brass (station roof) made by Maquetbarna (scale 1:400), 2009.

▲ View of the same architectural model. The model can be dismantled so the roof of the bus station can be removed to reveal the interior structure.

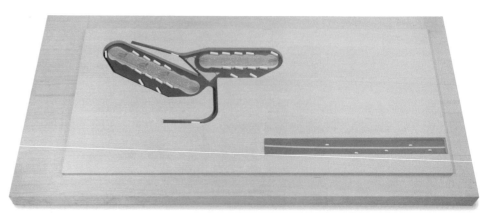

▲ The top of the model is also removable to allow the lower structure of the bus station to be seen.

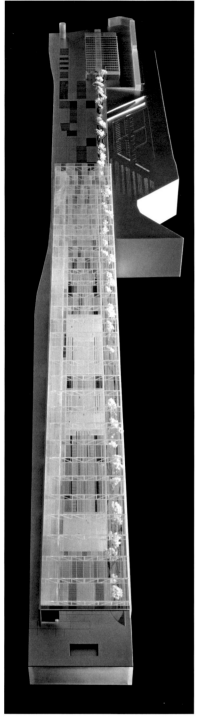

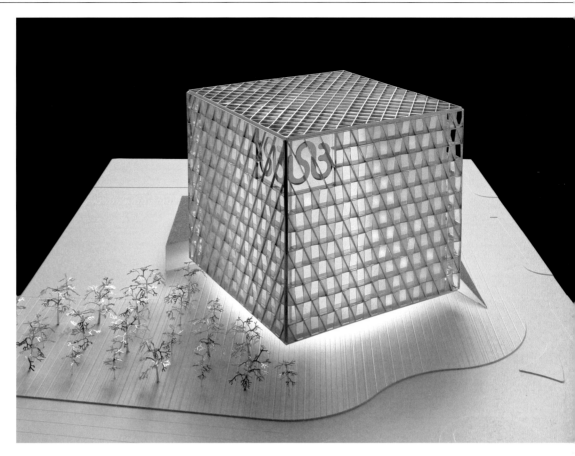

▲ Design for the headquarters of the company Seda de Barcelona, Carlos Ferrater, architect. Architectural model of acrylic and chromed brass (structure of the façade) and with interior lighting, made by Maquet-barna (scale 1:200), 2009.

◀ Design for the intermodal station in Florence, Italy, Carlos Ferrater, architect. Architectural model of acrylic and with lighting, made by Maquet-barna (scale 1:400), 2005.

◀ Detail of the model above showing the lighting underneath.

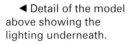

▲ Design for the headquarters of the World Health Organization in Geneva, Carlos Ferrater, architect. Architectural model of acrylic on a base with preexisting topographical representation in gypsum made by Maquet-barna (scale 1:400), 2006.

# Glossary
*and note on measurements*

## a

**Acrylic.** A plastic (polymethyl methacrylate, or PMMA) with excellent transparency and optical quality. It is light and very resistant to blows, ultraviolet rays, and the elements. Its greatest inconvenience is that it is easily scratched.

**Adhesive.** A product used to glue together two objects or fragments through mechanical attachment. It can be natural or synthetic (the result of chemical synthesis).

**Architectural model.** A three-dimensional representation of an object, building, or environment at a reduced scale.

## c

**Computer graphics.** This term refers to computer-generated images using special computer software. These images represent three-dimensional objects, environments, and scenes as realistically as possible.

**Contour lines.** A graphic convention used to represent the reliefs of terrain. These are the lines that join the points that are at the same altitude above sea level.

**Covering.** A layer of material that completely covers the surface of any part or piece of the model.

## d

**Design phase.** The intermediate phase of an architectural project, follows, the draft phase, in which the general characteristics of the architecture are precisely defined, adopting specific solutions. This is the phase prior to implementation.

**Display case.** A box of a clear, transparent material that is placed over the model to protect it from damage and dust, allowing the model to be viewed. In architectural modelmaking, the most commonly used display cases are those made of acrylic; this material has similar characteristics to glass but is lighter in weight.

**Draft phase.** The first phase of an architectural project in which the essential aspects and general characteristics of a building are displayed, without excessive detail.

## i

**Implementation phase.** The last phase of the architectural project, after the design phase, in which the design is fully implemented. All final details and characteristics are determined during this final phase.

**Isolines.** Contour lines.

## l

**Laser.** An acronym for light amplification by stimulated emission of radiation. The device is based on an effect of quantum mechanics called stimulated emission, which amplifies a beam of monochromatic coherent light.

**LED.** A light-emitting diode, commonly called an LED, is a semiconductor device which produces reduced spectrum light and functions using a continual current. In architectural modelmaking, LEDs are chosen to light models because of their small size and the amount of light emitted, as well as their durability, strength, and ease of assembly.

## m

**Massing.** Massing models offer a representation of the global image of the architecture, as well as the general forms and volumes of the buildings without details, using pieces in which only the volume has been represented. These are the most common architectural models in the draft phase.

**Methylene chloride.** Also called dichloromethane, methylene dichloride, or DCM, this is an industrial solvent and paint thinner that is used in architectural modelmaking to join acrylic. It is applied to the joins and acts by superficially dissolving the acrylic.

**Model.** A copy or original archetype that is used as a pattern to make something, imitating it or reproducing it.

**Module.** A piece or collection of pieces that is repeated throughout a building, e.g., a façade, in order to build it more cheaply and easily.

## r

**Representation.** An image of something that represents or replaces reality, and also the idea of reality that is being thought about.

## s

**Scale.** The size or proportion of a plan or architectural model, in other words, the proportions between the dimensions of its parts and the parts of the building or architectural project and the area that it represents. Scale describes the reduction ratio between reality and the architectural model that represents it.

**Scale ruler.** Also called an architect's scale, this is a special triangular ruler on which different scales are represented. It is used for measuring and converting scales.

**Section.** The representation of the profile of a building cut along one plane to reflect its structure and interior layout.

**Slope.** The incline of a wall or terrain.

**Stand.** A construction—usually temporary—that is placed within a trade fair or market and is designed to exhibit and sell products.

**Structure.** The layout and ordering of the main parts of a building, or the parts that support it: pillars, beams, reinforcement, etc.

## t

**Topography.** A set of features that presents the surface configuration of terrain and the way it is represented. This is a scientific discipline that studies principles and procedures, with the aim of graphically representing the terrain with its natural and artificial forms and details.

**Track ballast.** A layer of broken or crushed stone that is spread across the surface of the ground. The ties are placed on the ballast and in turn the rails are laid and fastened on them. Track ballast offers stability, because it helps preserve the geometry of the construction and contributes to keeping the railway line in good condition.

**Translucent.** The effect produced when the surface of a transparent, usually clear material, like glass or acrylic, is rubbed with sandpaper or sandblasted so that the light transmitted through it is diffused.

## u

**Urban planning.** A term that describes the discipline of the study of cities; its main focus is the study and layout of urban systems. It also refers to all knowledge related to planning and executing the improvement, expansion, organization, and layout of cities, and the buildings and spaces that make them up.

## v

**Veneer.** To cover a support with one or several thin sheets of wood which are glued onto it with contact adhesive and then pressed firmly. The support needs to be prepared in advance for veneering.

**Note on measurements:** *The measurements for the projects in this book, originally published in Spain, were metric. The American equivalents added here are rounded; for the most accurate reproduction of the models shown, the metric figures should be used. Since materials available may be available in different forms in the United States, we have given the closest approximation to the sizes and types of materials specified.*

# Bibliography
## and acknowledgments

CONSALES, Lorenzo. *Maquetas. La representación del espacio en el proyecto arquitectónico.* Barcelona: Gustavo Gili, 2005.

KNOLL, Wolfgang, and Martin Hechinger. *Architectural Models. Construction Techniques.* Fort Lauderdale, FL: J. Ross Publishing, 1997.

MILLS, Criss B. *Designing with Models.* New York: John Wiley & Sons, 2000.

SARDO, Nicoló. *La figuraziones plastica dell'Architettura. Modelli e rappresentazione.* Rome: Kappa, 2004.

SUTHERLAND, Martha. *Modelmaking: A Basic Guide.* New York: W. W. Norton & Company, 1999.

UBEDA, Marta. *La maqueta como experiencia del espacio arquitectónico.* Valladolid, Spain: Secretariado de Publicaciones e Intercambio Editorial de la Universidad de Valladolid, 2002.

*The authors would like to thank Parramón Ediciones, and in particular Tomàs Ubach, for having entrusted us with this project. We would also like to give special thanks to Joan Soto and the whole team at Nos & Soto fotògrafs, S.L., for their dedication and collaboration, and to Núria López-Ribalta and Jaime Cases for their invaluable help.*

*We wish to express our gratitude too to the companies, institutions, and professionals who have helped produce this book and who have made it possible, especially*

*Xavier Gutiérrez;*

*Toni Martín: www.martinmodels.com; and Maquet-barna-QuantumLeap: www.arrakis.es/~quantumleap/*